White
Teacher

White Teacher

Vivian Gussin Paley

HARVARD UNIVERSITY PRESS
Cambridge, Massachusetts
and
London, England

Printed in the United States of America
10 9 8 7 6 5

Library of Congress Cataloging in Publication Data

Paley, Vivian Gussin, 1929–
    White teacher.

    1. Afro-Americans—Education.   2. Kindergarten.
3. Classroom management.   I. Title.
LC2771.P34   371.9'7'96073   78-9841
ISBN 0-674-95185-9 (cloth)
ISBN 0-674-95186-7 (paper)

Designed by Mike Fender

For Irving

Foreword

JAMES P. COMER, M.D., *and* ALVIN F. POUSSAINT, M.D.

FEW PEOPLE CAN WRITE about serious subjects from a position of deep personal involvement and remain objective, insightful, entertaining, and wise. But Vivian Paley has done it in *White Teacher*.

Not since Sylvia Ashton-Warner's *Teacher* has there been a book so singularly significant to all of us concerned about quality education. Like Ashton-Warner, Paley understands that children are surging, creative, energetic people who must channel their aggressions and acquire the skills of their society. She recognizes too that the classroom is a template, shaping children for adult life in a changing world. But Paley goes beyond Ashton-Warner.

Paley does not believe in preparing children for a society that is so recognizably imperfect. That would be a task filled with contradictions. In *White Teacher* she examines and challenges society's values as reflected in the classroom, not in a self-righteous and condemning way, but through the examination of her own prejudices, blind spots, and shortcomings that inevitably result from growing up in this society. She does not reject all that is old or traditional or lead a crusade against injustice as young educators are often prone to do. Nor does she discard proven techniques by substituting "modern" innovations for their own sake. In her microcosm—the classroom—she helps her kindergarteners develop the intellectual and social tools necessary to face the world as it is and to move it toward what it should be. She nurtures them to be able to survive society's hardships and helps them to feel that change can occur—that children can live and grow together despite differences in race and social origin.

There is no more important task in America today. We are disturbed that more than two decades after the Supreme Court decision barring school segregation, schools, particularly in the North, are becoming more segregated than ever before. We bemoan school violence between groups that are racially and economically different. We despair because people who are different cannot live together in peace. But these facts should not surprise anyone. Where in the rearing of children do we ever help them learn to appreciate and respect both differences in themselves and others? Without this emphasis we cannot expect to have a peaceful, stable, and thriving heterogeneous society.

In spite of the urgent need, many of our schools run from discussions of racial and social differences. In the media, stories of racial conflict or even ethnic awareness activities are minimal. And in our classrooms textbooks replete with racial and sexual stereotypes are still being used. Until our own book, *Black Child Care,* there was no comprehensive guide for black parents to help their children grow up with pride in their cultural uniqueness in the face of negative societal attitudes and practices. Until Paley's *White Teacher*, few writers gave teachers a model for a systematic examination of their own prejudices or provided them with strategies to respond in constructive ways to the natural and healthy inquiries of children from various backgrounds.

Paley is effective in helping people appreciate themselves because she respects human differences but is always mindful of human similarities. It was a relief, and a basis for hope, to discover that she didn't start out that way; that she grew to be comfortable with differences through a personal commitment to fairness and a determined effort to understand herself and culturally different people. The role of the black teacher in this book and Paley's openness in receiving help and insights from her are particularly significant. Too often white teachers ignore or demean the potential assistance they can gain from black parents and teachers in understanding the black child. Paley does not fall into the trap of perceiving differences in black children as deficiencies. Born a Jew in a world controlled by Gentiles, she has sensitivities that may be greater than those of many people. But the fact that she was able to grow and change is what is most significant.

Paley's most beneficent trait is her ability to utilize unspoken questions and nonverbal cues as an aid in understanding her pupils. With the help of games, play, drawing, reading, and writing, she is able to use her perceptions to relieve the children's hidden fears and uncertainties. No area of inquiry is forbidden. All of the transactional relationships in her classroom are opportunities for social, intellectual, and psychological growth. One can almost feel her pupils gain confidence and pride themselves as the stories unfold with suspense and vitality.

Vignette after vignette tells it like it is for the child, his or her classmates, and the teacher—what they thought and did about it and the outcome. You will laugh at the things which make children all over the world funny and cute—good intelligence limited by the fact that they have not lived as long as we adults, have not gained the kind of understanding of events that we have, but have developed their own "funny" formulations of the way the world works. You will occasionally be outraged by their hostility, threatened by their aggression, and warmed by their humanity and desire to be cooperative. Paley's understanding that her role is to teach, that love and compassion are not enough, prevents her from losing teacher-child boundaries and slipping into the destructive role of an overaccepting do-gooder who gives all and expects nothing, or who even tolerates abuse to the detriment of the growing child. She remains capable of setting limits and confronting children with misperceptions, misunderstandings, contradictions, and self-destructive behavior. Above all she demonstrates that you can maintain student discipline with a warm, fair-minded, democratic but firm style.

Yet one must be reminded that Paley was teaching in schools that were well-supported, primarily middle-class, and predominantly white. She had the materials and administrative help to make her work effective. Her classes were not overcrowded and they had a good cross-section of youngsters. Often she was able to enlist the support of parents and other teachers. The physical and social deterioration of an inner-city school might have overwhelmed Paley. This is not said to deny her skills and ability, but to point out that effective teachers function best under conditions that support their teaching efforts. Many more teachers like Paley might emerge in our public schools if adequate economic and administrative support were given to the educational system.

As we read this book we were reminded of how important schools and good teachers are to a child and thus to society. Much of what is called bad behavior and social problems could be prevented or ameliorated if we had more classrooms like Paley's and if a larger number of parents and families functioned in the same way—with patience, understanding, and humanity. This book is not for teachers only, but for everyone concerned about the well-being of children. We hope that many people will read it.

Preface

"WHY DO YOU TALK so much about the black children?" The question comes from Elaine, who is a student teacher in my kindergarten class. We eat lunch together nearly every day and our conversation usually involves two themes: What does it feel like to be a teacher? What does it feel like to be a child?

Elaine continues: "I'll bet you comment three times as often about black children in this class, even though there are only ten blacks to twenty whites."

"Why do you think I do it?" The direction of authority is always revealed by who repeats the questions. Elaine tells me she doesn't know my reasons, but she thinks I feel less certain in my judgments of black children.

She is only half-right. My uncertainties about labeling behavior and intelligence in general have been exposed by my dilemmas concerning black children. My attempts to help black children feel more comfortable in a white environment have made me more aware of the discomfort every child experiences as he realizes he is being judged by someone who does not know him.

The child has already learned which of his characteristics are seen as weaknesses by those who take care of him at home. Suddenly a stranger called "teacher" is trying to find out not who he is, but what he knows. The further away the teacher is from the child's cultural or temperamental background, the more likely it is that the wrong questions will be asked. The child instinctively knows the questions are inappropriate but soon figures out that *he* must be the one who is inappropriate. Thus he begins the energy-consuming task of trying to cover up his differences.

Each year I greet thirty new children with a clear picture in mind of who shall be called "bright" and who shall be called "well-behaved." Ask me where these "facts" come from and I will probably refer to my professional background. Yet I doubt that the image I carry of the intelligent, capable child has changed much since my own elementary school days. It has been intellectualized and rationalized, but I suspect it is much the same, and that image was never black. The few adult blacks I knew were uneducated laborers and I never played with a black child. During my first ten years of teaching, in a southern city and an eastern suburb, I had a total of three black children.

What then did I bring to this integrated school in which I have taught for the past five years? My luggage had "liberal" ostentatiously plastered all over it, and I thought it unnecessary to see what was locked inside.

The narrative in this book describes my experiences with black children. In the beginning it was more comfortable to pretend the black child was white. Having perceived this, I then saw it was my inclination to avoid talking about other differences as well. Stuttering, obesity, shyness, divorced parents—the list was long. My awkwardness with black children was not a singular phenomenon. It uncovered a serious flaw in my relationship with all children.

As I watched and reacted to black children, I came to see a common need in every child. Anything a child feels is different about himself which cannot be referred to spontaneously, casually, naturally, and uncritically by the teacher can become a cause for anxiety and an obstacle to learning.

The role of the teacher changes. From the often negative function of judge and jury, the teacher can rise to the far more useful and satisfying position of friend. Strangers hide feelings and pretend to be what they are not. Friends want to know and talk about everything. It is a good environment in which to learn.

It has been useful for me to record my thoughts and feelings during this span of five years. We all have the need to explain ourselves. Teachers seldom have the chance to do so. Yet our behavior in the classroom becomes an important part of the "hidden curriculum." My story, like anyone's story, is a morality tale. You do not share your experiences without the belief that there are lessons that have been learned. And these lessons are invariably obvious ones.

The black child is Every Child. There is no activity useful only for the black child. There is no manner of speaking or unique approach or special environment required only for black children. There are only certain words and actions that cause all of us to cover up, and there are other words and actions that help us reveal ourselves to one another. The challenge in teaching is to find a way of communicating to each child the idea that his or her special quality is understood, is valued, and can be talked about. It is not easy, because we are influenced by the fears and prejudices, apprehensions and expectations, which have become a carefully hidden part of every one of us.

White
Teacher

1. THE BLACK CHILD appeared on the second Monday of school. I would be the only teacher in the school to have a black child. I had the feeling I was getting her because I was most likely to treat her properly. This, of course, was ridiculous. Alma Franklin would be in my class because I was the kindergarten teacher and she was five years old.

I had grown up in Chicago, but my first teaching job was in the south. All the years that I lived in the south I taught in white schools. This was before desegregation. I told everyone that I wanted an integrated class. Society forced me to teach white children, I insisted. I became the school radical, and had fantasies about visiting colored children in their homes.

Even so, when I moved back north, it was to a white suburb. I was still teaching white children. The guilt was there. It had to be explained. Look, these kids have to be taught too. It's not as if I was teaching in a private school. This is a public school.

Alma was in my class for two weeks and still she had not spoken to me. She would not look at me, and she would say nothing but "Ysm." She liked the children and their activities from the start. Much of what we did seemed unfamiliar to Alma, but she watched carefully and copied the other children quickly and well. From the first day, Susan gave Alma the role of baby in the doll corner. "Now, Alma, you be the baby. I'm the mother." Pale blond mother and dark brown baby. It gave me a good feeling to watch. There is no prejudice in this classroom. These children see no color difference.

Alma spoke with the children, but her voice was soft and her speech so slurred I could not understand a word. The children responded as if they knew her meaning. Whenever I approached, Alma stopped talking and lowered her eyes. I was puzzled and hurt. Why is she afraid of me? Nothing I did helped Alma feel comfortable with me. As children do in such circumstances, the others began to interpret Alma's needs for me. "Alma wants another cookie," "Alma can't do the puzzle," "Alma needs more finger paint."

I kept watching myself as I tried to relate to Alma. I knew that the relationship of a white teacher and a black child could be traumatic, but it was intolerable that a black child should fear me. I decided to call Alma's mother. She worked for a Mrs. Rossman.

"May I speak to Mrs. Franklin?"

"Mrs. Fran . . . ? Oh, Louise. Louise! Pick up the phone." A different voice said, "Who could be calling her?"

The extension was lifted. "Hello?" came the soft drawl.

"Mrs. Franklin? This is Mrs. Paley . . . I'm Alma's teacher."

"Yes, ma'am."

"Mrs. Franklin, could I make an appointment to talk about Alma?"

Silence.

"Uh . . . Mrs. Franklin, it's nothing serious. Alma seems so shy." My voice was shaky. "If I knew more about Alma I could help her relax more and talk more in class."

"Ain't Almy bein' good?"

"Oh yes. Oh heavens yes. Alma's very good. She's a lovely child. We all like Alma. It's just that she's so shy with me."

"Miz Paley, y'all tell her what's needed. Ef'n she's bad, she'll get a whippin'."

"No, no, not bad. Certainly not bad. Uh . . . ok, fine. We'll talk again soon. Alma's a very nice child. Yes, indeed. Bye now."

"Yes, ma'am."

I'll give her more time, two weeks is such a short time. I looked up Alma's record. No previous schooling. Age five and three months. Parents separated. Iberville, Louisiana. The report was filled out in a very uncertain script. Alma and her mother live at the Rossmans'. Housekeeper. How did they get to the Rossmans? Should I speak to the Rossmans? No, just wait, see what happens.

"Alma, you look like chocolate pudding." We were all sitting around having snack time. Paul repeated, "Just like chocolate pudding." A few children laughed. Most paid no attention. I became rigid and pretended not to hear. Alma was looking at Paul with interest. She did not seem to feel insulted. Is it an insult or not? I couldn't decide. Do I react? To what? She does look the color of chocolate pudding. But he shouldn't say that! You never say anything like that to colored people.

I continued drilling myself. Why didn't I say something? What am I supposed to say? Say noth-ing. Alma's already uncomfortable with me. If I say anything to draw attention to her blackness she'll never talk to me. Who can I talk to about this? Never mind, I'll handle it myself. I don't need help.

Monday was the day Alma got hurt. She was watching some boys build with blocks. I had never seen her play with blocks. Suddenly she picked up a block, walked over to the tower of blocks and, with a huge grin, put hers at the very top. The tower came crashing down, one block hitting Donald. Red-faced, he jumped up and pushed Alma as hard as he could into the closet door. He yelled, "You bad brown doody!"

Alma's head caught the edge of the door. She screamed in pain and grabbed for her head. When she saw blood in her hands she began to wail and shake. I ran to Alma and frantically hugged her. I rocked her back and forth as she moaned. I could feel her rage and fear. Poor baby, what was she doing here in this sea of white faces?

The words rushed out of me. "Alma baby, my pretty colored baby. Now hush, y'all. Hush, Alma honey." I heard my voice; it had a sing-song tone that sounded like the Negro women I used to hear from my window in New Orleans. It was soft like Mrs. Franklin's.

Alma stopped crying. She looked up at me and

put her tiny dark hand on my face. Then she put her thumb in her mouth and gently laid her head down on my shoulder while all the children watched.

2. I THOUGHT A LOT about Alma that summer. She had left before school was out. Alma told me, "Mama, she miss Mama Bea and Papa." There must have been some Louisiana Cajun influence in Alma's family, because she always used the pronoun after the proper noun ("Mama, she . . ."). Alma and I had become friends. On her last day in our kindergarten she made a card for me on which she printed eight words she had learned to read. She put each one inside a flower.

I did not have my talk with Mrs. Franklin; perhaps we both avoided a conference, and their early departure took me by surprise. I managed quite well to make no reference in front of Alma to anything that was different about her. What I had once blurted out under emotional stress, I could not repeat under the cold light of reason and rationalization.

For example, I got some books about black children. One was called *Whistle for Willy*, by Ezra J. Keats. I wanted to ask the children, does Willy look like anyone in our class? Or maybe ask, would you like to have Willy for a friend? What if someone said, no, he's not the color I like? What if someone said, he looks like Alma, and it embarrassed Alma? What would be my purpose in all this?

I read the book. It's nicely done, and the children

liked it. A little later, on our way to the all-purpose room to do some tumbling, Leo said to me, "All the children in Willy's book are poor."

"Why poor, Leo?"

"People with brown skin are poor."

I instinctively glanced around to see where Alma was. She was up in front.

"Leo, I know some people with brown skin who aren't poor."

"But they look poor," answered Leo, and he ran on ahead.

In September I had two black children in my class: Valerie Wood and Fred Barton. I still taught in the part of town that was all white, but the school board was trying to put some black children in the white schools. Valerie and Fred came from a kindergarten that was overcrowded. There were still no other black children in our school. Both children had been born in New York City. Valerie's father was a bus driver and Fred's worked in a local fish market. They lived on South River Road, which had six blocks of black families.

On the first day of school Valerie announced, "My daddy said, don't play with Fred 'cause Fred is bad." "I ain't bad," Fred informed us, but he did not sound too sure.

One by one that first week all the teachers came by to check out the two black children. That is not what they said they were doing, but that was what they were doing. Fred had quickly become part of an aggressive little group of seven. Every time someone walked in, these restless children could be found grabbing, yelling, arguing, pushing, and running. The six white children in the group received scant notice, but a comment was always made about Fred. "You've got your hands full with him." "Shouldn't he be in a special class?" Nothing was said about Valerie, who had discovered the art corner the first day and hardly left the painting table for six weeks. Only Fred drew an immediate and consistent response. He already had a reputation. Actually, John, Keith, Raymond, David, Michael, and Denise behaved just as Fred did. The differences were mainly color and speech, and Denise and Keith both had infantile speech patterns. So we get down to color.

I sorted out this information and presented my observations at the first faculty meeting the following Monday. There was a vigorous discussion. Our conclusions were these: more than ever we must take care to ignore color. We must *only* look at behavior, and since a black child will be more prominent in a white classroom, we must bend over backward to see no color, hear no color, speak no color. I did not argue against this position because I could not justify another.

We had a fairly good year. Fred settled down and became a good person to play with. A few boys began to invite him to their homes. Valerie, who was so concerned about being good that she was afraid to try out new activities, inched her way into the doll corner and entered the world of make-believe. "Pretend we're teen-agers . . ." became one of her favorite ways to begin.

The Bartons and the Woods were friendly and co-operative parents. Never once did we mention the racial difference between their children and everyone else in the school. Mrs. Wood came to the first PTA function, but did not return.

There were "incidents" during the year that left me troubled. I began making a list of those I couldn't handle, the first of many such lists.

1. Valerie said to Fred, "Go 'way. Don't want you for a partner. I want someone white."
2. We made pudding, vanilla and chocolate. Daniel said, "Valerie and Fred have to eat chocolate. That's their color."
3. We were looking at a set of pictures, part of a social studies curriculum. A playground fight was pictured. Joanne said, "The poor boy is helping the other boy." All the children wore jeans and T-shirts, but the "poor boy" was black.
4. Keith and Fred became friends. One day Keith said, "Fred, the front of your hands is clean but the rest of you is dirty." Fred answered, "I ain't dirty." Keith looked worried. "Not really dirty. Just colored darkish." Fred looked at his skin and said, "I'm sunburned." Keith looked happy. "That's right."

When Valerie told Fred she wanted a white partner I was silent. I did not know what needed to be said to help both of them. If she had told Fred his painting was scribble-scrabble I might have said, "Fred, Valerie thinks you're painting scribble-scrabble. Is that what you're doing?" Then Fred could have told us how he felt. But I could not transfer this matter-of-fact, nonjudgmental description of what was being said when race or color was involved. When Denise became annoyed with Valerie and told her not to sit next to her because this was not a "brown" chair, I responded with equal annoyance. "Valerie may sit wherever she wishes, Denise. Please don't tell people where to sit." I saw I was purposely avoiding the part about the *brown* chair.

It was clear to me that I was unable to mention color in the classroom. When I was little we never referred to the color of the cleaning lady's skin. Of course we would not say "nigger." But, in her presence, we would never say colored, black, brown, skin, hair, maid, or Negro. In other words, we showed respect by completely ignoring black people as black people. Color blindness was the essence of the creed.

3. THE OUTSIDE WORLD was struggling to get in and shake up our comfortable suburb. We organized a Human Rights Committee and had meetings and raised money for civil rights causes. We decried the absence of blacks in our community. We picketed apartment buildings in the center of town that did not rent to black families. Most of us who picketed lived in houses in all-white neighborhoods.

Some people worked hard to try to bus fifty or

sixty inner-city children into our schools. The plan was defeated in a referendum. Some people attempted to convince the community of the value of building a low-income garden apartment development in the middle of a wealthy part of town. This plan was also defeated. Both plans would have brought a small number of black children into white classrooms.

In our self-contained classrooms we were trying to integrate some new materials about blacks into the curriculum, if not the blacks themselves. There were more pictures of urban middle-class black children and adults who did not look poor. We began trying to say "black" instead of colored or Negro, but few of us could use the word "black" comfortably. I had not yet referred to racial differences in front of a black child or his parents. I was only able to do this at the Human Rights Committee meetings. The meetings were, for me, a substitute for any real relations with black people, and there was a sort of professional language that we all used at those meetings.

In September Valerie and Fred moved back to New York, and I moved to a Midwestern city. The public schools were not hiring new teachers at that time because of economic problems and strike threats, so I took a job in a private integrated school. By integrated I mean my first class of thirty had nineteen whites, eight blacks, and three orientals.

The racial proportions of the student body at the school were about the same as in my class. Almost all the teachers were white. The administration was white, and there were some black secretaries and custodians. In other words, a white integrated school.

Still, my new school delighted me. I was intoxicated by the variety of children in my class. Finally I had a really integrated class. Eight black children will have a strong enough identification just among themselves. Not only that, but having met some of the black parents, I felt that their racial self-image scored pretty high. These were mostly middle-class, urban, educated blacks. The combination of college degrees and Afros reminded me of my own doctor father with his prayer shawl. The image said to me, ok, I've made it in your culture, but I'm different and I haven't forgotten that.

Three things happened the first month of school which made me reopen the whole problem of black children and white teachers. The first was a conversation with my mother. We were having one of those leisurely "remember when" kinds of talks. I was trying to explain how I had felt being one of the few Jewish children in my elementary school, and I told her of my fears of being an outsider.

She was astonished. She told me that more than a third of the school was Jewish, and insisted that I was a very confident child and proud of my heritage. It was difficult for her to accept my memories. I could see why I never told anyone how I felt when I was a child. Even now, I was feeling guilty. I also saw that having a dozen other Jewish children in the class didn't make being a Jew more acceptable

in that room, because not one of the teachers accepted us as Jewish children. They insisted we were
all just children, which meant we were all Gentile
children since that was the only kind of child they
thought about or talked about. The more my parents
provided me with roots in my own culture, the
more I felt my differences from the culture of the
school. Failing to be recognized as a Jew, and knowing I was not a Gentile, I did not know what I was
at school. Receiving good grades relieved some of
my guilt but did nothing for my anxieties at
Christmas and Easter, surrounded as we were by
Christian symbolism and pageantry.

The second thing that happened was a meeting I
had with a black parent in my class. Mrs. Hawkins
told me that in her children's previous school the
teacher had said, "There is no color difference in my
classroom. All my children look alike to me."

"What rot," said Mrs. Hawkins. "My children are
black. They don't look like your children. They
know they're black, and we want it recognized. It's
a positive difference, an interesting difference, and
a comfortable natural difference. At least it could be
so, if you teachers learned to value differences
more. What you value, you talk about."

But it was Michelle Parker who made me respond
to her immediate need. Michelle, black and viva-
cious, pointed to a picture in a book I was reading
to a small group and said, "I wished I looked like
her." The "her" was a blond, pink-cheeked girl. I
could have easily ignored this. Maybe Juli Ann,
white and plain, wished she looked like the girl in

the book too. When I was little, I know I would have wanted to look like her. But Michelle had a special, obvious reason. I knew I must say something.

"Michelle, I know how you feel. When I was little I also would have liked to look like this little girl. She doesn't look like anyone in my family, so I couldn't have looked like her. Sometimes, I wish I had smooth brown skin like yours. Then I could always be dark and pretty." Michelle looked down at her skin. So did everyone else. I don't know what she was thinking. But I knew the feelings I had expressed were true, though I did not know it until I spoke.

4. "DON'T TALK TO ME. I don't have to listen to no white lady."

The boy covered his ears and squeezed his eyes shut. His black skin glistened in the sun and there was a fine spray of sand covering his short thick hair. Everyone in the sandbox was staring at Steven Sherman. He opened his eyes a crack. "Don't nobody white look at me. Don't talk to me. You stink." He kicked a bit of sand at the children, but none of them moved. "Fuckers!"

I was annoyed at myself for feeling angry. Was it the part about the "white lady" that bothered me, or the language? I was not comfortable with words like "fuck" or "shit." I am more relaxed about it now than I used to be, but at that time, coming from a five-year-old, it shook me up.

A few years back I was in a sex education in-service course for teachers, and I progressed a fair amount in handling my feelings about these words. I even got to the point where I could use them on occasion. But when a child hurled them out at me, I was hurt. However, I was more interested in the other part of Steven's outburst. The idea of a black child using "white" as a dirty word was new to me. I pretended to myself that I was personally indifferent to the attack. All that mattered was helping Steven handle these explosive incidents that kept recurring for him.

But the truth was, I felt attacked. How could this be? Was I reacting to this affront to my authority as a teacher or to my authority as a white? I asked myself these questions during the following days, but I really knew the answers. If Steven had said, "I won't listen to you," this would have been an ordinary situation. I was, of course, reacting to the hostile use of "white" by this black child.

The funny thing was, I knew there would have been only one thing worse for me. If he had yelled "Jew" instead of "white" I would have been more upset. This thought gave me courage. I do feel more Jewish than white. My ego seems to be tied up in Jewish images and insecurities. I have always acted as if the conscious or subconscious feelings of white superiority were part of the gentile world. "They" think they are superior to blacks. "They," never me. But Steven Sherman sees me only as a white lady. I can't crawl into my Jewish role. I must react as a white, so Steven will know I'm not worried about our differences. But I *was* reacting as a white and I *was* worried about our differences.

I ignored the sandbox incident, other than to warn him not to throw sand again. It was time to go in anyway. I managed to compliment Steven during the walk to the classroom on how well he was keeping in line, and that seemed to take the edge off his tensions, and mine.

Ten minutes later Steven threw a block at John's head, barely missing. There was no way to ignore Steven. He was a disruptive, angry, and disagreeable child who hit children too often. And he happened to be black. If only he were white. The factor of skin color was getting in the way. I couldn't ignore it as I had in the past, because Steven kept bringing it up. This person was a "fuckin' honky," and someone else was a "white motherfucker." But the cursing was not the primary problem. Children were being hurt. If Steven were to remain in the class, he had to stop hitting and bullying the children. He was nicer to the black children, but even they were afraid of him.

I had been reading some books dealing with various behavior modification techniques. I attended a few workshops and was impressed by the approach. It suited my feelings about teaching. So I began a consistent program of positive comments and reactions to Steven. I watched him like a hawk and, every time he did anything constructive, helpful, or even barely friendly to others, I commented.

"Steven, I was just noticing that you gave Tommy the block you didn't need. That was helpful and friendly."

"Sharon is happy because you're sharing your crayons."

"You fixed up the paints so well, Steven. Someone else can use them right away."

"I see you didn't fight about the chair. That was a friendly way to act."

Steven loved the compliments. He looked around for me when he did something worthy of recognition. "I'm letting Jimmy use the little cars. I don't need them." The trouble was that he was also growing more aggressive toward some of the children. Part of the behavior modification strategy is to ignore as much as possible the antisocial behavior of the child. Of course, each harmful act must be stopped. But that's all you do. You stop it and give it no further attention. The idea is that the abundance of attention given to positive behavior will diminish the negative behavior.

This made sense to me. I especially liked the approach because I sensed my own anger at Steven as he continued to monopolize so much of my time, and these positive techniques helped me cover up my negative feelings. But it was not working. His moments of extreme hostility seemed to be increasing. What was I doing wrong? Did he sense my anger?

I tried a gimmick, involving a little blue book, the kind used for college exams. I showed Steven the book and a set of rubber stamps with designs on them. Each page would have a date at the top, and we would record every helpful act. I would write it down and he could stamp it. Steven was delighted with the blue book. I also continued my practice of paying minimal attention to his aggressive acts once they were stopped or prevented. At such times I would say, "Don't throw blocks," and then remove Steven from the area in which the harmful behavior had occurred.

And still his behavior got worse. I decided, impulsively, to hell with this business of ignoring hurtful behavior. This is nonsense. It is unnatural, and he knows it as well as I do. It is confusing him. He must be punished each time he hurts someone.

I took Steven aside during a calm interval and told him I was very unhappy about all the hitting he was doing. I thought he would stop it because there are so many things he does well. Now, however, when he hurts someone, he will have to sit alone, away from the class, in a "time-out" chair, and do nothing for ten minutes. I showed him the chair, and he nodded.

He wandered around the room, looking at the chair. I became involved in writing down a story Jan was dictating. Suddenly Steven pushed Jimmy down and began kicking him. I jumped up, grabbed Steven, and dragged him to the chair. He would not come by himself and he would not remain seated. He screamed furiously. I said nothing but held on to both his arms and sat next to him. He struggled and tried to kick me. I said, "Steven, don't even think of kicking me. I can't ever let you do that. I have to make you sit here because you won't do it by yourself. Every time you hurt someone you must sit here."

I told the children, over his screaming, that Steven needed me to sit here with him. They must have understood that I was upset and Steven was upset, and we were trying to work something out. They stayed away from us and their play was subdued. They were upset too.

This was a Monday. We did this twice on Monday, and twice on Tuesday. On Wednesday, Steven sat on the time-out chair by himself with no complaint. After that, he stopped hitting children. I had won because of superior strength and size. I was not sure what was won and what was lost.

5. STEVEN NO LONGER hit children, but his abusive language increased. Even so, I knew our relationship was better. He would let me put my arm around his shoulder now, and he had never allowed that before. No matter what his emotional problems might be like, I wanted him to feel this school was a safe place to be in.

I used every chance I had to mention the words "black" and "white." I don't mean that I carried on philosophical discussions about the brotherhood of man—nothing was in the abstract. I simply was trying to divest these terms of their negative meanings in Steven's mind by showing him, and the others, how easy it was for me to talk about being white or being black. And it was starting to be very comfortable; it was almost therapeutic. I felt a profound sense of relief.

"Steven, that orange shirt looks good on your brown skin."

"Charlene, your Afro is so soft and round. It feels good when I touch it."

"My light skin will get darker if I sit in the sun like this, but I doubt if I can make it as dark as yours."

"Here's a new book all about black children. Look, the man who wrote the words is white like me and his wife, who is the artist, is black like Charlene and Steven and Jimmy."

The more I talked about being white and being black, the less Steven used these terms in anger. One day we had a young visitor. Jerry was black, but his skin was lighter than mine. The total impression was of a black child, undoubtedly of mixed parents. Steven asked me, "Is Jerry black or white?" I said, "I don't know. We could ask."

Steven went up to Jerry. "Are you black?"

Jerry answered, "I'm half black and half white. My daddy is white and mother is black."

Steven was elated. "We've got the book they wrote!" He ran to the bookshelf and brought out our new book. Jerry carefully looked at the picture on the dust jacket.

"No, my dad doesn't have a beard. They're not my mom and dad."

Steven was thoughtful for awhile. Then he said to me, "Now we know two families that have black and white people in the same family."

Steven's periods of constructive behavior and normal conversational speech were increasing, but when he was frustrated in any way he still muttered or shouted bad language. Ironically, Steven was helping me overcome my severe reaction to these words. The more I heard them, the less important they became. As Steven's swearing lost some of its emotional content for me, I was able to concentrate more on his feelings and less on mine. Nonetheless I still felt the language was as inappropriate in the classroom as hitting is.

I tried ignoring Steven when he swore. I gave him immediate attention when his voice was gentle, and turned my back on the rest. This had the same effect as ignoring the fighting. He continued to swear, furious with me for ignoring him. He could always provoke me to the point where I would finally yell at him, "Cut it out! That's enough of that talk!" Then Steven would return my anger, sulking and glowering for about ten minutes. When he began to hum to himself, he was approachable again.

I did not want to punish Steven for using these words. His words did not hurt the other children; they hurt me. But I also felt they hurt Steven. The angry sound of his swearing built up a wall around him, isolating him from us.

One day I said to Steven, during a quiet time, "Hey Steve, would you mind not saying 'fuck' so often? I know you like to say it but it really makes me feel bad. Look, how about this? Say it twice each day, ok? And you can say 'shit' two times also." I had not planned this. It just happened. I kept thinking, what a strange thing to do. The next day, he called Sam and Edward the usual names. I said to him, "I counted twice. You called Sam a 'fuckin' honky' and Eddy a 'motherfucker.' That's all until tomorrow."

Soon Steven was telling me when he reached the limit. I don't know why this approach worked with Steven, but it surely did work. It may have been because I was no longer angry. In fact, I was getting to like Steven a lot.

By the end of the week, Steven had eliminated almost all the racial epithets from his school vocabulary. The occasional profanity that escaped was short and honest and easily ignored by everyone. More important were the new behaviors Steven was trying out. He was still easily frustrated. His anger erupted from some deep source. His eyes would suddenly glare, his face would become frozen in sullenness at a moment's notice, and his whole body would slump into a stiff position. But he was starting to come to me with arguments and complaints. He was using different language to express some of his feelings.

"Teacher, Andrew keeps using my glue. I don't want his hands on my glue. I hate him." He was mad, but in control.

"Steven, that glue must be shared. It's the only jar left. Now, you use it for three minutes, then Andrew may use it for three minutes. Take the three-minute timer so you and Andrew will know when your time is up."

Steven was usually able to accept solutions like this. But not always. There were times when I sensed a rigidity that could not be handled within a classroom context, when he was unable to make the smallest concession. Then I had to say, "Steven is not able to share now the way he did yesterday. He'll feel better soon." And the subject was dropped. (One must see the realistic limitations of any situation.)

An important insight I received from the behavior modification people had to do with helping children observe their own behavior and especially their own growth.

"Steven, remember when you used to throw things at people and hit them? You've learned how to talk about what's happening to you now. You don't hurt your friends anymore."

"Remember when you used all those words I didn't like? Just now you were mad at Sam and you yelled, 'Stop that! Leave it alone.' You said plain ordinary words and he understood exactly what you wanted."

I have not mentioned Steven's parents up to this point, because I wanted to trace the series of events within the classroom. I was maintaining regular contact with Mr. and Mrs. Sherman, and found that for the first time I was able to communicate with black parents in an honest and open manner. I described Steven's behavior, without being clinical or judgmental. What I told the Shermans is pretty much what I have written here. I explained just how I was trying to use behavior modification principles, what was working and what was not. I was involving them, not in placing blame or criticism, but in the way I would involve a colleague. We were examining the situation, trying to break it down into component parts, and seeing together what kinds of things might lead to growth and what kinds of approaches seemed fruitless.

I was able, toward the end of the year, to suggest a psychiatric evaluation. It was, in fact, Mr. Sherman who asked, "Don't you think we ought to try to find out why Steven gets so angry so often? It might get worse when he gets older." I said I thought this was a very positive approach. I told the Shermans that many parents find it hard to seek expert opinions when it comes to emotional health, though they have no such problems when the child has a chronic stomachache.

6. I HAVE ALWAYS IDENTIFIED with children who feel different. Children like Steven can become catalysts; my own distant painful feelings of being different were coming to the surface.

I remembered a boy named Jeff. He was very much like Steven, except that he looked like me. He hit children, he screamed, he destroyed things. His anger probably matched Steven's, but his swearing vocabulary was limited to "doody" and "stinky." I was in my early twenties then, and I considered quitting. This was my first real teaching job, at the local Jewish community kindergarten. I hated Jeff, I hated teaching, and above all I hated not being able to admit any of this to anyone. Since I lacked the skill to deal with Jeff, the courage to admit my feelings, and the wisdom to seek help, the year was a near disaster for me.

And yet I muddled through, because basically I felt at home. I was in a Jewish school, with a Jewish staff and Jewish children. I did not have to think about my skin color or Jeff's, nor did I have to react to any other differences. I felt young and ineffectual, but I never felt under attack as a human being. I never felt I had to explain myself.

My next job was in a small, rural public school. The school was all-white, blue-collar, lower-middle-class, in a section on the Mississippi River. Now I began to feel some differences. For one thing, I was a northerner. Second, my background was Jewish, middle-class, urban, liberal. Up to now I never had to worry about what I said or how I said it. The first time I heard a child say "nigger" before, I reacted quickly.

"Don't say that! That's a bad word. It hurts people's feelings." Even when the child said, "My daddy says it," I had no conflict. "Well, I don't ever want to hear that word. You can say 'colored' or 'Negro,' but not the word you said." Of course I never said the word.

In my new school words like "nigger" and "coon" were part of the language of some of the children and teachers. My noble posture disintegrated. My credentials suddenly disappeared. As one Jew talking to another I could say anything I felt like saying. Now *I* was the outsider. I was afraid to say anything disapproving to anyone.

I reacted to all aspects of classroom behavior except to the colloquial language of the deep south. It completely unnerved me each time a child used the word "nigger," but I was silent. I'm sure my annoyance came out in other ways, but I didn't give much thought to buried anger in those days.

One day I was having a casual conversation with a father. He was a huge, red-faced, jovial man. I remember looking at his hands and thinking they were the largest, fattest hands I'd ever seen. Suddenly I realized he was saying, "so he jewed me down . . ." I stopped listening. I had never heard this expression before. But my own reaction was far more shocking to me. My first thought was, I hope he doesn't know I'm Jewish . . . does he? How could I have been so cowardly? I felt deep shame. I could not discuss this or any of my other inadequacies with anyone. I kept thinking of things I should have said. It was on my mind for weeks and then was gradually forgotten.

7. ARLENE WAS IN Steven Sherman's class. She was the smartest five-year-old child I'd ever had. In almost every category you could name, she was first. She read and wrote like a bright second-grader. She was enormously friendly and had fun playing anything with anyone. She was equally adept in the doll corner or in the block area, and she did puppet shows that actually had plot and character development.

One day she began writing a newspaper. She called it the "Daily News" and spent two days collecting stories. She went around telling everyone she was a reporter from the "Daily News" and did they have any news for her, especially good news?

Mary Anne said, "My mother has exams today at medical school. When I woke up today she was studying."

"That's strange," Arlene said. "My mother is also studying for her exams in medical school. This will be a good story for my newspaper."

She asked how to spell "medical" and "exams," and rushed to her office, which she had set up in a corner of the room. Twenty minutes later, the story was finished. There was a picture of two women, one white and one black, both holding books, paper, and pencils. The caption read, "Two mothers are going to be doctors." This was followed by a brief story. "Two mothers of two girls in the same school and the same class are taking exams in medical school. One mother is white and one mother is black and they are both going to be doctors. The End."

Arlene was black. I was glad she was in this class, because Steven was there. In other words, if the most difficult child in the class was black, then I wanted the most outstanding child to be black too.

I told myself that the reason I felt this way was that I wanted the white children to have this balance so they would not develop a stereotype of blacks based on Steven's behavior.

Now, why should I have felt this way? In a class of thirty, we had ten black children. There was only one Steven. The others had the usual mix of characteristics which depend on sex, size, coordination, and general maturity.

The year before, Steven's counterpart was white. The brightest child was also a white boy. It never would have occurred to me to be glad he was white. Not once did I wonder how the black children might feel about the most threatening boy in the class being white. It seemed I was confident in the staying power of whites and I did not need to worry about the small percentage of white problem children in every class. I was uncovering a very disturbing idea. My level of expectations for whites as a group was obviously higher than for blacks.

But what kind of prejudice was I exposing, racial or economic? Arlene's black parents and Mary Anne's white parents were educated and upper-middle-class, lawyers and doctors. Certainly my expectations were no lower for Arlene than for Mary Anne. I was sure of that.

But look at Charlene and Kathy, both black, and both with parents whose schooling stopped at high school. They now held low-level white-collar jobs. Were my expectations lower for these girls, and if so upon what was that based?

Charlene and Kathy were restless and had short attention spans. They enjoyed running around, in and out of activities, making a lot of noise and teasing boys. When pinned down, they showed above-average intelligence, a great deal of humor, and very positive feelings about school. Their language, unlike Arlene's perfect grammar and articulation, included a lot of "ethnic speech."

"Leave me be, girl. You ain't my friend no more."

"If I tells your mama, she gonna whip your tail."

"My mama never whip me, girl."

Both girls had a fine time. And so did everyone who listened to them. I was amused by this frequent banter between them. But it was not *my* language. This was not the language of children from educated families, who live on educated streets and have educated conversations at home.

One day I found out that Kathy's older sister was considered one of the brightest students in her class. I began to look more closely at Kathy, and I felt my expectations changing. I was butting into Kathy's frivolous play more, and encouraging longer conversations with both Kathy and Charlene. I observed that during these talks with me, and during play with white children, their speech was getting to be middle-class school speech.

"Getting to be?" No, not getting to be. I began to realize that many of the black children regularly used different speech patterns when playing with each other and when playing with white children or teachers. They moved in and out of this speech with ease. They had no problems here. *I* had the problem. Actually, I made the same sort of instant transformation with certain Jewish friends. The Yiddish expressions would appear, the inflections, the broken English of the immigrant, all of which resulted in good feelings and frequent laughter.

Why didn't Arlene ever speak in the jargon of the "brotherhood"? Well, I have many Jewish friends who don't either. I don't know why in every case, but certainly one must have some regular exposure to the ethnic speech and it has to provide a kind of comfort of belonging in its usage. My most pleasant childhood experiences involved people who were immigrants. This speech soothes my soul and sounds like music to me. But obviously not to all my friends.

And so it must be with Arlene and other black children I know who never seem to lapse into another speech structure. Then again, maybe they do, but not in front of a white teacher. As a child, I would never have wished to draw attention to my differences before a non-Jewish teacher. It may seem that I am overdoing my comparison of Jewish feelings and black feelings. But I am talking about feeling different. Perhaps coming to terms with one kind of difference prepares a person for all kinds of differences. At least this is the way it was for me.

8. THE FIRST DAY of school is filled with suspense. Here are thirty strangers who will become your intimate family. While you are watching them, they will be cautiously watching you. Nothing can be covered up. They instinctively know what you mean, whether or not you say it.

Each child wants to know immediately if he is a worthy person in your eyes. You cannot pretend, because the child knows all the things about himself that worry him. If you act as if you like him, but ignore the things he is anxious about, it doesn't count. The child is glad you are nice to him, but down deep he figures if you really knew what he was like, you'd hate him. So your liking him without knowing him just makes him feel guilty.

This was the first day of school.

"Mrs. Paley, are you Jewish?"

I looked at the name tag to see who was asking the question. It seemed out of context. Barbara Marcus.

"Yes, Barbara, I'm Jewish."

Barbara spent the first week asking children if they were Jewish. She did not ask black children, but she asked oriental children. She often asked people more than once.

Barbara made me uneasy. Is it healthier when a black child asks if someone is black? Why does that sound good? What was different about Barbara and her question? Maybe I still preferred that Jews not draw attention to themselves. On the other hand, I would have been concerned if a black child kept up this inquisition for a whole week. But a black child usually can see who is black; Barbara could not tell by looking.

Sitting at the table at snack time, Barbara would suddenly say, "Everyone who's Jewish raise your hand." Or, she'd be at the painting table: "If you're Jewish come to my side of the table." Something had to be done, but I kept avoiding the problem.

One day Barbara announced she was organizing a Jewish club. She let everyone in who agreed to be Jewish, except black children. She told them only white people were Jewish.

That night, a concerned black parent called me. "Mrs. Paley, Ellen is crying because she's not Jewish. Could you please explain what's going on in your classroom?" I exploded with laughter and explained to Ellen's mother, "Mrs. Loam, we have a girl named Barbara who is having an identity problem. She told Ellen that black people can't be Jewish."

"Did you tell her about Sammy Davis, Jr.?"

"Well, no. I don't really want her to make any converts." I was laughing again.

"Mrs. Paley, what should we do about Ellen?"

I became serious. Ellen's mother saw no humorous aspect to her daughter's dilemma. I told her I wanted to think about the problem and call her back.

"But what should we do about Ellen?"

"Look, don't worry about Ellen wanting to be Jewish. Just treat it lightly. It's no different than if she came home and cried for a new doll her friend has."

I called back in an hour and asked Mrs. Loam if Ellen had a favorite Sunday school song, perhaps an African song. She suggested "Caney Mi Macaro," which was on our Ella Jenkins record. I told Mrs. Loam I would try out a few ideas and talk to her again soon. I was going to need her help.

At 8:45 the next morning, Barbara was busy making Jewish stars out of construction paper. There were only five Jewish children in the class, but she had already passed out eleven stars, each with masking tape, ready to wear. I called everyone to the piano. "Barbara has been thinking a lot lately about being Jewish. I know a song with Hebrew words that some Jewish children like Barbara learn in Sunday school. 'Shalom Chaverim.' It means 'hello friends.' " We sang it twice and Barbara said, "Sing it again. I love it." So we sang it again.

I asked Ellen to bring the Ella Jenkins record. "Ellen's mother told me about a song they love at Ellen's Sunday school. It's not a Jewish Sunday school, because they're Methodists. Ellen goes to a Methodist Sunday school. This song is from Africa." Ellen jumped up. "My teacher is Mr. Raymond. He used to live in Africa. Can I put on the record?" "Caney Mi Macaro" has a strong beat, perfect for rhythm sticks. We made a lot of noise and a little bit of music.

After music, Barbara finished making her stars. She passed the rest out and gave one to Ellen, who looked very pleased. I was tempted to lift it from Ellen before she took it home, but decided to place some faith in the Loams, hoping they would be more relaxed about it than my parents would have been had I brought home a cross from school.

I began calling parents. Our school has quite an international population. This class had families from Pakistan, India, China, and Panama. In addition there were fairly recent immigrants from France, Germany, Hungary, and Italy.

I explained that we were collecting our own songs and would try to learn each other's music. I asked the parents to write out the song and send it to school. Or better yet, to send the music or a record. Otherwise the children could sing the song for the music teacher, who is skilled in writing down music.

For a while we sang our family songs every morning, intermixed with a lot of American folksongs. When we sang a Hebrew or Yiddish song, Barbara had a chance to tell everyone that she is Jewish. She had stopped asking people to label themselves. A few of the other Jewish children began to talk about themselves. None had ever joined Barbara in her crusade. Andy told us that his grandfather lives in Israel. "In Israel, the ambulance has a Jewish star on it," he said, as if he could not understand how this could be so.

Vasanti, from India, brought a picture of her cousin sitting on an elephant. She also had a song about an elephant named "Chichi" which sounded as if she had made it up. We sang "Chichi" over and over and pretended to be elephants swinging our trunks. Vasanti was delighted. The next day she brought us a book about a baby elephant. She pointed to a girl in the book and said it was her cousin and that the photographer was her uncle. This impressed everyone. Every day children looked up Vasanti's cousin in the book.

I had been caught up in white-black differences and Jewish-gentile differences. My own background made these very real for me. Differences that had no emotional overtones for me, but were real enough to each child, were being neglected.

Carol Shen is Chinese. One day we were looking at a book about how babies are born. There is a page at the end that had a drawing of six babies. The racial origin of the two white and two black babies was clear. The babies intended to portray oriental and "other" were perhaps not so clear. I asked the children to point to the baby that looked like their own baby pictures.

All the white children pointed to white babies. Half of the black children pointed to white babies and half to black babies. The oriental and Middle Eastern children vacillated between all types, but most finally chose white. Carol would not choose. She got up and left the group. She took a book and inched her way into a corner near the piano. I suddenly realized that Carol was not at ease in this class. From the beginning I had been impressed by her reading and writing abilities, and her general maturity. If she had anxieties about her differences, they did not appear on the surface.

David Hoo-Yen was the only other Chinese child in the class. He had told us that his father was teaching him to read Chinese before he learns how to read English so that he wouldn't get mixed up. David and Carol played checkers every day at snack time. I sat at their table and printed the Hebrew word for "boy." "David, do you know how to write 'boy' in Chinese? Here it is in Hebrew."

"Oh, sure. I already know lots of Chinese words." He printed "boy" in such big letters it filled up the page.

"Anyone like to copy a very big Chinese word? David wrote it for us." Barbara was the first to run over. "This is the very first time in my life I'm writing in Chinese," she told us. Barbara always liked to explain what she was doing. Though she was not pasting stars on people any more, she still seemed to be involved in an identity search. Her latest passion was drawing people with brown skin. She made a picture of herself with brown skin.

I wondered if Barbara would reorganize the Jewish club every time she entered a new class. Her chances of getting another Jewish teacher at this school were slim. There were even fewer black teachers, one oriental, and no Middle Eastern or Spanish teachers. What if Steven Sherman's first teacher had been black? Wouldn't his kindergarten year have been less traumatic?

Certainly his most serious problems would have existed with any teacher and any class. But Steven's initial confrontation had been, "I don't have to listen to no white lady." A black teacher might have gained his trust sooner.

I had no answers. How much does it matter if a child cannot identify ethnically or racially with a teacher? Does it matter at all? If the teacher accepts him and likes him as he really is, isn't that enough?

How is Carol Shen to be shown that she is accepted? David Hoo-Yen seemed to have no problem being Chinese in a white school. Carol evoked memories of myself as a young girl. She avoided any activity or discussion that had to do with her own people and culture. She was spending more time reading and less time playing. This is a cause for concern. Kindergarten is a time for play. A child's good feelings about himself and others come through play, not reading.

Carol was avoiding us. She was using books and paintings to isolate herself. Her manners were always correct. She helped children when asked, and she cleaned up properly. She smiled, but it was the smile of someone who is afraid to frown, someone who wants to avoid attention.

I asked Dr. and Mrs. Shen to come in for a conference. They were from Taiwan, and both had heavy accents. There were quite a few of Mrs. Shen's words I could not catch. Often Dr. Shen would provide the missing word. They began voicing their concern about Carol. Dr. Shen's mother had come for a prolonged visit from Taiwan, and Carol had begun behaving very poorly at home. She was rude and sulky. She refused to speak Chinese to her grandmother, who spoke no English. Carol, it turned out, spoke Chinese fairly well.

I told the Shens that Carol's behavior was not unusual in an American-born child of immigrants. The cultural differences can be confusing. I had a cousin who never brought PTA notices home in hopes that her mother would not come to school and reveal her foreign accent and peasant clothing to the teacher.

Mrs. Shen's eyes reddened and she said something to her husband in Chinese. Dr. Shen said, "My wife thinks it might have been better if we had not come to America." My grandmother used to say things like this as she saw us growing distant and resentful.

"Mrs. Paley, this is not your problem. It has nothing to do with school," Dr. Shen said.

"But it's part of Carol. It's tied up with everything." I told them what was happening at school. "How about coming for a visit, with your mother-in-law? Let's try it out." Mrs. Shen agreed to come, but with no enthusiasm. That evening Dr. Shen called. "Carol is quite upset. You can probably hear her crying. She does not want her grandmother to come for a visit."

I asked to speak to Carol. "Honey, lots of people don't want visitors in school. If you change your mind, let us know. It's perfectly fine either way."

"Ok, Mrs. Paley," was the tearful reply.

One can move too fast. Sometimes preparation is needed. I had been wanting to involve parents more in our activities but had been too lazy to do anything about it. It does require planning. If you want children to feel comfortable with their parents coming to school, and parents to feel they belong here, you must plan for it.

Cooking is good common ground, I thought. Maybe Carol's mother or grandmother enjoy cooking. But first let some other parents come in. Carol does not want to appear different. Right now she would rather copy others.

I asked Vasanti's mother first because I knew she was writing a cookbook. She showed us how to make little triangular pies filled with chopped meat. Each child filled his own "sandiwich," as Vasanti called them. Mrs. Kanrayyals always wore a sari, and Carol seemed fascinated by it. She kept touching its filmy pastel material. Mrs. Kanrayyals noticed this and said she would show us how she puts on the sari. Vasanti's usual somber face was lit up with smiles and giggles. From time to time she kissed her mother's hand and her mother always returned the kiss on the top of Vasanti's head.

Ellen's grandfather, a baker, came several days later. He is at least 6 foot 6 inches tall and with his tall white hat he looked like a beautiful black giant. He made corn bread and corn pones because Ellen asked him to. This was a professional operation. He had four tables going at the same time. We served everything warm and with jam and margarine.

The following week David's mother, Mrs. Hoo-Yen, made won ton. As she began to roll out the dough, Carol ran over. "My grandmother makes this. My grandmother makes won ton!"

I asked Mrs. Hoo-Yen if she could teach us something in Chinese. She and David, in unison, repeated a saying of his grandmother. "When the Kitchen God sees how good and kind I am, everyone will be happy." The Hoo-Yens say this at the time of the Chinese New Year. David and his mother went over it again, one word at a time, and we all followed. Barbara said, "This is the first time in my whole life I'm speaking Chinese."

The next day Carol brought in a little statue of the Kitchen God. She showed it to me, but then put it in her cubby without showing it to anyone else. Later Carol played in the doll corner with Mimi and Lisa. Her statue was sitting on top of the kitchen cabinet. Barbara came in, insisting, "I'm the mother!" Everyone objected because Lisa was already the mother. Carol said, "You can be the grandmother coming for a visit. You have to bring this to me for a present." She handed her the statue.

Several days later Carol came up and whispered, "My grandmother doesn't speak English." Ah, she told her secret.

"Do you understand when she speaks Chinese?"

"Yes, and I can even talk in Chinese." She ran off to the doll corner to play.

The elder Mrs. Shen returned to Taiwan without a visit to school. But on Carol's birthday her mother came and brought some Chinese candy they had made at home. It's a bit salty and tastes like plums. Carol told everyone at her table, "This is real Chinese candy."

9. JANET ALBRIGHT ARRIVED at the right time in my life. She was the best student teacher I ever worked with and she was black. Janet was not a young college girl; she was forty and had raised four children. She taught in a day care center for seven years, and now she wanted her B.A. with teaching certification so she could teach in the public schools.

 Janet was more sensitive to the feelings of children than the most experienced teachers I know. She instinctively understood the nature of objectivity and involvement. Her involvement did not encourage dependency and her objectivity could never be interpreted as indifference.

 She liked every single child. This is a great comfort to children, having a teacher who likes everyone and knows how to show it. When you have a teacher who likes some and not others, you must keep maneuvering for her approval. This interferes with the more important business of learning to relate to your own peers.

Stuart was in our class that year and he had a bad stutter. Stuttering, like skin color, is a characteristic most teachers prefer to ignore. Even after I could comfortably discuss color, I could not easily refer to a child's stuttering. I would look intently at the child and not let anyone interrupt, even in the natural way children always interrupt each other. I felt as though I was holding my breath.

Janet, by her example, showed me that I was afraid of the stuttering. My behavior revealed an inability to accept this stuttering child. After she had been in our class a few days, Janet was reading a story about a boy going to the Central Park Zoo in New York. Stuart excitedly tried to say that he had been there, but got stuck on the word "my" and could not extricate himself. Janet said, "Stuart, I see you have trouble with certain words, like 'my.' Some people call that stuttering. When you get older you'll figure out what to do about those words. But we don't mind waiting for you to say them. Not a bit. Take your time."

Larry was in the group listening to the story. "No, we don't mind. Not a bit," he repeated. Susan picked it up, "Sure. Just take your time." I realized what was going on. Janet had shown everyone it was all right to talk to Stuart about his stuttering. The message they had got from me was that it was not all right. And to Stuart, she was saying, in effect, "You don't have to try to keep this problem a secret."

Janet was interested in Stuart's problem, for one of her own children stuttered. She would say things like, "Stuart, you're having trouble with 'give' right now. Try saying, 'let me have it' or 'I need it' instead of 'give it to me.' " She was showing him that the stuttering did not have to control him. He could manipulate a little, change a few words, make a game out of it. She was not acting like a speech therapist. She was just putting herself in his shoes and figuring out what *she* would do if she stuttered. He knew that and he felt good about it.

Another nice thing Janet did was to let the girls fool around with her hair. She wore a big Afro. Very often black girls love to sit and comb the long blond tresses of white girls. I see this every year. There's nothing wrong with this, but it was good to see white girls combing Janet's hair with her special comb. Curiosity about hair works in both directions. White children wonder how thick, kinky hair feels. And Janet's obvious pleasure in her hair and her good humor about herself must have helped some of the black girls who had anxieties about their hair and color.

Janet's first day with us happened to be the day before Martin Luther King's birthday. During the morning I described an incident from Dr. King's childhood and told the story of Rosa Parks and the Montgomery bus boycott. I had been telling these stories since Dr. King's death, but now it seemed as if I was showing off. Look at me, Janet. Look how enthusiastic I am about Martin Luther King. I was beginning to blame her for my uncertainty.

After class, Janet said, "I like the way you told those stories to the kids. Were you self-conscious because I was there?" Her question surprised me. "Why do you think so?" I asked. She laughed, "Oh, I don't know. I've been in so many self-conscious situations myself, I always can see it in someone else."

"Yes, I was, as a matter of fact. Would you have felt this way talking about Judah Maccabee?"

Janet thought for a minute. "I don't know. Who's Judah Maccabee?"

I burst out laughing. "We'll get Barbara to educate you." I told her the story of Barbara's Jewish club while we ate our lunch.

The next day was King's birthday. At piano time Scotty reminded me, "You said we could act out about all the black people sitting in the back of the bus and the lady said she wasn't going to do it."

I asked Janet to take over and help the children organize the performance. She had indicated that she was especially interested in dramatics and role playing.

Scotty said he wanted to be Martin Luther King, since it was his idea to do the play. Michael, who is black, objected. "Martin Luther King has to be black. Scotty isn't black."

Janet said quickly, "Well, now. I think it's real nice that Scotty wants to pretend to be black like us. It wouldn't be fair not to let him. Mike, you be Dr. King the second time we do the play. A good play should always be repeated."

Janet made sure that Clarice (black) got to be Rosa Parks and Seth (white) the bus driver. Then she helped the children fix the chairs up to look like a bus. Here is the play, verbatim, as the children made up their lines on the spot:

ROSA PARKS: Here's my money.
BUS DRIVER: Go sit in the back.
ROSA PARKS: There's no empty seats in the back.
BUS DRIVER: Then you better stand.
ROSA PARKS: No indeed. I won't, you can't make me. I'm sitting right here.
BUS DRIVER: No, only white people sit in front.
ROSA PARKS: You're bad. I'm not paying attention to you. I'm tired. I'm sitting down. See?
BUS DRIVER: Ok for you. I'm calling a policeman. ("Oh, we forgot a policeman. Teddy, can you be the policeman?")

POLICEMAN: What's going on here?

BUS DRIVER: She won't go to the back of the bus.

POLICEMAN: Ok, come to jail.

MARTIN
LUTHER
KING: All right, no one who is black rides the bus. We don't like them any-more.

              (most of the children get off the bus)

BUS DRIVER: Now we don't have enough people on the bus.

KING: Promise you won't ever be mean to black people again?

BUS DRIVER: Ok. Everyone can sit wherever they want. Especially Rosa Parks. ("Hey, bring her out of jail.")

              (everyone gets back on the bus)

BUS DRIVER: Wait, nobody paid me. Never mind, you can all have one free ride.

Janet seemed so relaxed and confident with me and with the children that it took several weeks for me to notice how different her behavior was with other teachers. She withdrew and was almost totally silent. This made me even noisier than usual in a protective reaction.

When I asked her about it, she said she didn't feel comfortable with most white teachers. "They either avoid talking about race like it was a plague, or else they look at me *only* when black kids are discussed as if the ghetto is the only thing I know anything about. I feel absolutely paranoid when I'm with most white teachers. Not the kids, just the teachers."

This was the first time I had seen Janet angry. But I didn't want to drop the subject: "I'm not trying to challenge your feelings, but is it possible that white teachers are self-conscious with a strange black teacher? The way I was the first day?"

"Maybe. But I just always have the feeling they are behaving in such a fake way with me. Of course," and Janet was laughing now, "they behave in the same fake way with the kids too." She just couldn't stay mad for long and, besides, she liked the discovery she had just made.

One of the kinds of incidents which always gave me a sinking feeling was one in which a white child deliberately rejected a black child. This happened one day in Janet's presence and she seemed to have no trouble handling it.

We were taking partners so we could walk to Boland Pond. Barbara said in a loud voice, "I don't want Ellen again. She always wants to be my partner. I want someone white."

Janet walked up and put her arms around both girls. "Ellen, Barbara feels like walking with someone who looks like her. Sometimes people get that feeling. Can I help you find another partner for this time?" Ellen chose another white girl for a partner and nothing more was said.

When we got to Boland Pond, I sat next to Janet. "Frankly, I was surprised at your response back there in class."

Janet said, "Believe me, it's the only way. Guilt

feelings never bring about an improvement in behavior. I see you handle things this way all the
time. Why are you surprised when I do it?"

"Because I expected you to feel just a little bit personally attacked."

"Sure, I felt that way. But I know the way to make
friends and influence Barbara is not to make her feel
lousy about herself. Look at them. She and Ellen are
kissin' cousins again."

When I heard there would be a first grade open-
ing in our school the following September, I urged
Janet to apply for the job. My motives were partly
selfish. I liked being with Janet. Her experiences
and my experiences blended well, and we had developed a relationship conducive to exploring each
other's feelings about people and things. There
were very few teachers with whom I could do this.

More important, our school needed Janet. We had
only four black teachers in the primary grades, but
almost one third of our children were black. I don't
mean we needed Janet because it would look good
to outsiders. She was a superior person and skillful
with children. She would bring with her much-
needed experience that could be shared with white
teachers—that is, if we could get Janet to feel comfortable with the faculty.

Janet vetoed the idea. "I'm not cut out to be the
company 'black.' I belong in the inner-city schools
teaching black children. If I'm as good as you say,
let those who need me the most have me."

"But, Janet, these children need you too. You believe in an integrated society. Here's where you can

plant some seeds. And you've told me how much you enjoy working with the different kinds of children in this school."

"Oh, sure. I love these kids." Janet's voice became very soft. "They're so alert. So eager to communicate ideas and discover new things. I want to see if I can create this kind of atmosphere in a ghetto school."

She frowned. "And I'll tell you something, Vivian, *you* ought to be in one of those schools too. These kids don't need you as much as my kids do. You tell me how much a sensitive black teacher could accomplish here. Well, I'm telling you how much a sensitive white teacher could accomplish in a black city school. Why don't you think about that for a while?"

I do think about it. I don't know if Janet is right. This school is an exciting place. But perhaps the real challenge in education today is the one Janet is seeking. Not perhaps. It *is* the real challenge. Why do I feel I'm not yet ready? Am I afraid of being the outsider again?

10. APPROXIMATELY 60 PERCENT of the children at our elementary school come from the faculty and staff of a local private university. The others are from the general population. The immediate neighborhood is the prototype of a university community, an integrated middle-class area where most of the university people live, the majority of whom are white.

Our extended neighborhood is one of remarkable diversity and represents the total gamut of black urban life. There are rich, middle-class, and poor. But the poor cannot afford the tuition at our school.

So, if you attend this school and you are white, your family is probably connected somehow with the university. This is also true if you are oriental or Middle Eastern. But if you are black, you are seldom from the local establishment. Your parents may be professionals or in business, and you live in a mostly black neighborhood.

John William Clayton and Mitchell Schneider met on the first day of school and became best friends. They began building a road with blocks at the same time and simply joined up.

"Put your blocks over here. This side needs more long blocks," directed John William.

"Ok," said Mitchell.

"Let's play with blocks all day," said John William.

"Ok," said Mitchell.

"My name is John William. Don't call me John. Call me John William. John is my daddy."

"Ok," said Mitchell.

The next day Mitchell waited near the door for ten minutes until John William arrived. As soon as he saw John William he put his hand in his pocket and took out a tiny metal car and gave it to his new friend.

"Good, we can use this," said John William. "Let's make the road again."

Mitchell and John William played together every day. They had their snack together, they moved their cubbies next to each other, and neither one became involved in an activity until the other was ready to join.

The boys were alike in many ways. They were both small for their age, and neither had brothers or sisters. Their fathers were teachers. Mitchell's father was a professor of sociology at the university, and John William's father taught history at a public high school. Both mothers were social workers.

The most conspicuous differences between the boys were color and movement. John William was black and Mitchell was white. John William was always moving and his way of moving was uniquely his own. He cartwheeled around the room. He leaped, he pirouetted, he catapulted his lithe figure through and around over everything he did. He sat still only at story time, and even then his outer stillness barely covered his inner drama. He so identified with the characters in the story that all their emotions could be read upon his face.

Mitchell was very quiet and, but for his attachment to his friend, he might have gone unnoticed for a while. He moved self-consciously, as though he were afraid he might be taking up too much space. He looked around before sitting down on a chair, to see if someone else had been about to take it.

As it was, Mitchell did not go unnoticed, for the visual contrast between the two friends was quite remarkable. John William was ebony black, had huge dark eyes, and a close-cropped head of tight curls. Mitchell was pale and fragile-looking. His eyes were shaded by thick blond lashes and his hair was more white than yellow, worn shaggily down his neck.

An invisible band seemed to connect the two boys, and the band was always pulled in both directions. John William would pull Mitchell into the rhythm of his restless movement, and Mitchell would pull John William to slow down, to sit and watch and speak softly.

Christmas vacation was almost here, and neither boy had yet played with anyone else. They accepted each other's idiosyncrasies without question. Sometimes when walking in line John William would suddenly let go of Mitchell's hand and do a series of cartwheels in the hall. Mitchell would keep walking until John William returned and took his hand again.

Once a teacher came down the hall from the opposite direction. Startled, she said, "What are you doing, young man? We walk in the hall!"

Mitchell called out, "John William does cartwheels. Our teacher doesn't care." That Mitchell would speak to a strange lady was very surprising to everyone, because he hardly ever talked to visitors in our class.

Mitchell liked to sit at a table and draw pictures of great adventures. Sometimes he would recreate Batman and Superman TV stories, but usually he would make up his own characters who had weird names like "the ugly green slimey shadow" and were involved in rocket ships and explosions. Sitting was hard for John William and he was not too interested in drawing. But he developed a choreographic relationship with Mitchell's pictures. He would sit for a while and keep saying, "What's that? What's happening there?" and then act it out. When Superman dived off the burning building, John William would get on the table and jump off.

The boys did not see each other during the three-week Christmas vacation because John William went to North Carolina to visit his grandparents.

On the first day back in school a new boy joined our class. Robert looked like a second grader though he was not yet six. He was as dark as John William and his big Afro made him appear twice as tall. The first cartwheel of John William brought Robert running over.

"Hey, man. That's cool. Show me how you did that!" John William did a few more cartwheels.

"Hey, man, I'm going to try me that. Clear off the rug, you kids," said Robert, and he flopped around without success. "Take me a while to learn that," and his clumsy attempts made him laugh so much that the children standing around began to laugh too. Robert liked that and he flopped over a few more times for the benefit of his audience.

Then he put his arm around John William. "Hey man, what's your name? You and me is brothers."

John William looked over at Mitchell, who had been silent all this time and was at a table starting to draw. Then he asked Robert, "You want to make a road with me?"

"Naw, I'm going to build me the John Hancock building. You can help me if you want. You and me is brothers, now don't you forget," and Robert got busy with the blocks, confident that his new friendship was sealed.

Changes were soon apparent. John William was still friendly with Mitchell, but he began moving toward the other black children in the class, because those were the children Robert related to first.

Robert was like many other big, bouncy, five-year-old boys. He was the youngest of four brothers and he was used to a loud, competitive, brotherly, teasing relationship with children. He copied certain mannerisms from his big brothers that fascinated John William.

"Hey, baby, that's cool. Real cool. I dig it, man," he'd say as he sort of jitterbugged-walked in a way that reminded me of the zoot-suited Danny Kaye of long ago, hunched over, fingers digging down, saying, "Well, dig-dig-dig well all right." Robert carried it off beautifully, and John William was getting himself ready to try it out.

Mitchell watched it all as he drew his pictures. I began getting phone calls from his mother. Mitchell didn't want to come to school. He was complaining of stomachaches. He refused to invite any one over but John William, and now John William was playing with Robert every day after school. It turned out that they lived on the same street only two blocks apart.

It is very sad to be rejected by a best friend. Of course, it happens all the time with children, but

Mitchell didn't know that. He didn't know that John William had to try some new friends and that he himself would one day do the same thing.

Mrs. Schneider worked out a plan with Mrs. Clayton whereby John William would spend every other Saturday with Mitchell. This made Mitchell feel much better.

John William did not become as close to Robert as he had been with Mitchell. Robert was too sociable to stick to one person. He liked to play with lots of different children and, although he initially played with only black children, the first time a white boy invited him home after school, Robert integrated his social life.

John William also became quite popular. When children saw that he was no longer playing exclusively with Mitchell, they made room for him in all sorts of activities.

But Mitchell remained aloof. Most mornings he and John William did something together, usually in the block area. As soon as someone else entered the play, Mitchell left and returned to his drawing. John William no longer acted out the pictures, but once in a while he would sit next to Mitchell and draw his own pictures.

On Mitchell's birthday he chose John William to help set up tables for the party. This is the conversation that took place.

"John William, remember when we were best only friends?"

"We're still friends."

"But not best only friends."

"My daddy says I should have lots of friends."

"John William, do you only like black people now?"

"I like my mommy and daddy best and they're black."

"But do you like white people too?"

"Sure I do."

"From now on, will you always be my partner when we go someplace?"

"All right, I'll be your partner."

"Is Robert really your brother?"

"No, he just pretends."

"Ok."

Now that Mitchell had given his relationship with John William a more definite status he seemed more content. Perhaps it was the feeling that he was not entirely helpless in preserving a friendship he valued.

I had been encouraging Mitchell to dictate stories to go with his pictures so I could read them to the class at story time. Robert began giving Mitchell's stories the kind of admiration he had given John William's cartwheels.

"Mitch, baby. That's a cool story. How come you make such good pictures? Hey, man, show me how to do that!"

Robert's enthusiasms were infectious. He was always intrigued by the skills of other children. His good-natured appreciation of the talents he observed was good for the ego.

Mitchell gladly demonstrated his drawing for Robert. Whereas John William had liked to perform what was already created, Robert directed the production.

"Hey Mitch, Batman and Batgirl have to be in the Batmobile shooting at the bad guys. And Robin has to be in the hideout with the Kryptonite."

Nothing was beyond Mitchell's ability. If the picture didn't work out, he would scribble black and red crayon over everything and call it a nuclear explosion. He was working like an artist with a vision. He was also behaving like a five-year-old who is on the verge of making a new friend. You take a shy child who has one friend. He does not necessarily believe he is capable of making another. But a child who makes two friends is on his way.

The next day Mitchell brought a note saying that Robert was to come home with him after school. Mitchell had gotten his mother to call Robert's mother and arrange for the visit.

All morning Mitchell played with Robert and John William. Out on the playground there were six children playing in Mitchell's group. There were two white children, Mitchell and Jenny; two black children, Robert and John William; one boy from Iran named Jafar; and Maria who is from the Philippines.

I wanted Janet to be here sitting with me so I could tell her again that this is the kind of group I want to teach. Not all white, not all black, just a lovely hodgepodge of everyone.

No, Janet would say. Not everyone. Where are the poor children?

This was something I could not answer. Are poor

children so different? Is it poverty that is the only significant difference after all? I envied Janet because I believed she was teaching in the front lines. I was back in my old quandary. When I taught white children I said I ought to be teaching black and white. Now I am teaching black and white children and I feel guilty because I am not teaching black children in the ghetto.

11. IT IS OFTEN HARD to learn from people who are just like you. Too much is taken for granted. Homogeneity is fine in a bottle of milk, but in the classroom it diminishes the curiosity that ignites discovery.

The class I had two years after Janet left opened up areas for me I had never even thought about. At the end of the first week I said to my principal, "This is the class I will write a book about called 'Everything I've always wanted to know about children but have been afraid to ask.' "

Claire Mireau, to begin with, helped me understand what play is all about because she had never played. She showed me how language can cease to communicate when a child has developed no sense of how she fits into a cultural setting vastly different from her own.

Claire's father brought her on the first day. They both looked worried. Mr. Mireau smiled a lot, but his eyes darted around the room. I wondered if he was counting the other black children in the class. Claire did not smile at all. She watched her father's face as he spoke rapidly to me in a West Indian accent. He explained why his wife did not come. She was expecting a baby soon and did not feel well.

When her father left, Claire stayed in the very spot he left her. She looked around the room several times and then fixed her stare on a group of girls in the doll corner.

"Claire, would you like to play in the doll corner?"

"He don't do it," she answered.

"Claire doesn't do it?"

Her reply came fast and although I heard each word I could not make sense out of what she was saying. The words were English words, but they seemed to be thrown together in some random fashion. I got the idea that she was talking about a baby and about something bloody.

Claire watched the children all morning but did not approach anyone or touch any materials. Nor did she respond to directions given to the group. When I led her to a table, gave her crayons and paper, and asked her to draw me a picture, she shook her head and repeated what she had said before. Again I heard "baby" and "bloody" and something about her mother.

What is this child about? Has she just come to this country? What language does she speak? French? Spanish? Has she ever been to school before? Even if I assumed she had just got off the plane, there were obviously factors other than language here. She did not seem to respond to nonverbal communication either.

Mr. Mireau arrived ten minutes before dismissal time and I began to question him.

"How long have you lived in America, Mr. Mireau?"

"Six years. We come her from Martinique."

"Then Claire was born here?"

"Oh, yes. She was born at this very hospital." He pointed toward the hospital which is on the same campus as our school.

"What language does Claire speak at home?"

"Claire speaks good English, pretty good French, and a little Creole. Her mother wants her to speak French, but Claire only likes English."

He spoke in the rhythmic cello-like tones of the Islands. I understood him very well, but I understood his daughter very little. As they left, I listened to Claire talking to her father. They were speaking in English and her father answered without asking her to repeat anything.

The days passed without much change in Claire. She began to smile a little and once in a while she would pick up a crayon and draw a big round face with barely recognizable features. She watched the children, but kept her distance. Most of the children ignored her, and a few black girls seemed to dislike her.

She had taken to sitting in a little rocking chair at the edge of the doll corner area. Some unpleasant remarks began to be directed at Claire by Karla and Rena.

"She's fat and ugly."

"Don't play with stinky Claire."

Claire did not react to any of this. I could not tell if she realized the girls were being unkind. When I saw that she would not respond, I interfered.

"Claire has been listening to some thoughtless and unkind words here. She doesn't seem angry, but I'm very sad. Claire is trying to get to know what being in school is like. She's never been in school before. I'm going to be my kindest to Claire. How about you, Karla?"

"Me too. Claire is not fat."

Ayana had not been unpleasant to Claire, but she added, "Claire's got pretty hair. Do you want to be the baby, Claire?"

Claire shook her head. "He is not baby," she said, and walked away.

She did not understand that they wanted her to pretend to be the baby. She did not know how to pretend. There is always pretending going on in the kindergarten, and I wondered if this could be the source of her confusion. But what does it mean when a five-year-old does not know how to pretend? Alma Franklin had come from a sharecropper's farm into an all-white northern class and she knew how to pretend.

Is this a cultural difference or a peculiar trait of the Mireau family? Is it possible that Claire has not observed children at play? Could there be some retardation here? Each day my conviction became stronger that Claire could not imagine herself as someone or something other than what she was and she did not know what someone named Claire does in school.

One day we listened to a record playing a rhythm that suggested jumping or bouncing. I bounced a beach ball up and down.

"We're all big, bouncy balls." I began moving up and down to the music. Claire stood alone among two dozen bouncing children.

"C'mon, Claire," I whispered. "Look at me. Up and down. Up and down."

"Me no can do dot."

I lifted her arms gently. She felt heavy and stiff. It took all my efforts to move her a single step.

I changed the record to the "Missouri Waltz" and exchanged the ball for a balloon on a string.

"I'm not a ball any more. I'm a balloon going up and down on a string." I looked at the children on the rug. Everyone had switched to slow motion. Their flashing eyes stayed on the large balloon floating up and down and they instinctively knew how it must feel to float in the air.

Except for Claire. She was an immovable rock among floating feathers. The others bubbled with laughter and Claire looked bewildered and sad.

She could not imagine herself as a balloon or a ball or a baby or a billy goat. The day before, we had acted out "The Three Billy Goats Gruff." Four groups acted out the roles of billy goats and trolls before I came to Claire.

"You are the littlest billy goat now, Claire."

She began shaking her head. "Ah no, no. Not me."

Could she not picture herself as a billy goat or did it seem improper for her to behave in such a manner? Several times I had the notion that she felt certain behavior was not right for her.

We took a walk to Boland Pond one warm day. Claire was walking with Sylvia. Sylvia did a lot of fighting in school but she had never bothered Claire. They had not chosen each other as partners, but neither one had a partner so I asked them to walk together.

Claire called out to me. I was startled because it was the first time I was aware of her calling me or anyone by name..

"Mrs. Paley, he squeezes me. Why he does do it?" She was surprised that someone would hurt her.

"Claire, you don't like it when she squeezes your hand. Sylvia, Claire wants you to stop doing it, so stop it."

This was Claire's first complaint. It achieved quick results. When Sylvia repeated her mischief, Claire complained even louder. I asked Claire to choose another partner and told Sylvia she must walk without a partner. Claire chose me and as we walked along she smiled a lot. She resembled her father when she smiled. Both were dark brown and had almost perfectly round faces. She was talking now in her father's tones, but her casual conversation was like a string of non-sequiturs.

While we were at the pond, Ayana slipped and skinned her kneee. It was Claire who informed me: "That black girl is hurt." Her response to pain was direct. But later, when I asked her to help pass out the milk, she hung her head and said something unintelligible about an uncle. She seemed to reject anything she had never done before as being improper. This would include most of our school activities.

My friend Christine works with children who have learning disabilities. I told her about Claire. Almost every characteristic I described, she said, could be a sign of certain kinds of disabilities. Claire's consistent misinterpretations of questions and her frequent inability to respond to group directions could be symptoms. So could her confusion over simple tasks such as moving individual parts of her body in a music activity or pretending to be some object or animal. The evidence was piling up. Once the label was suggested, there seemed no end to the data supporting the thesis. Christine was aware of this hazard. She cautioned that many children have some kind of developmental weakness, but in most cases other stronger abilities take over the underdeveloped function before the problem stage is reached.

What if Claire has no physical malfunctions? All of her questionable behavior, Christine felt, might be explained in terms of cultural confusion compounded by simple immaturity.

One day I set up a row of ten wooden cubes for Claire.

"How many blocks are there, Claire? Can you count them?"

She seemed to have trouble getting started. I took her finger and began, "One, two . . ."

She saw what was required. She counted slowly up to ten, touching each cube.

"Now, how many are there all together?" I asked.

She looked at me in the way she had when I asked her to be a billy goat. Then she smiled and began counting again until she reached ten.

"Fine, Claire. That's good counting. Now tell me, how many blocks are there in this row?"

Again she looked surprised. She stared at me for a moment and then counted for the third time.

I called my friend for an interpretation. "It's more of the same," she said. "Concept confusion."

"But what if she thought *I* was the one who did not understand? Here she counted to ten and I kept asking her how many there were all together. But she knew she had just told me. What if she was trying to explain it to *me?*"

"In other words," Christine said, "you suspect Claire thinks *you* have a learning disability!"

I laughed. "I'll tell you what I think. I'm going to forget the words 'learning disability' for a while. I'm going back to the beginning. Claire doesn't know how to play. A child learns primarily through play and here is a child who does not play. So we must teach her how to play. No more evaluating and measuring. Let her play for as long as she needs."

I called the Mireaus and invited them in for a conference. Mr. Mireau came alone and explained that the baby was due any moment and that his wife was resting. I told him I would like Claire to stay every Wednesday until 2:30. I explained that on

Wednesdays there are always three or four children staying for lunch and Claire would be able to play in a more relaxed atmosphere.

He was surprised. "Is she not doing well?"

"Claire needs more opportunity to play and to use our materials. She will understand more of what we do and say if she plays more with us."

"But everyday Claire tells me everything that happens. She tells me in English."

"At school she finds it harder to express her thoughts. Perhaps she's just not used to us. By the way, do you have any idea why she keeps talking about babies and blood?"

He laughed, but in an embarrassed way. "She saw a baby being born. On television. A real birth. She keeps thinking about it. Maybe because her mother is pregnant."

"You're probably right. Does Claire watch a lot of television?"

"Ah, yes. There is no one for her to play with, you see. We do not wish for her to play with the black children on our street. They do not play well. We tell Claire not to play the way they play. They are very bad."

Before Mr. Mireau left I loaned him a pile of books he could read to Claire at bedtime. Then he asked me if I knew any games he could play with her. I showed him four I had made using old trays and dice and egg cartons. He was very interested.

"I can make these easily. And I'll make you this egg carton game out of wood. It will last longer."

"You like to work with tools?"

"It is my great joy."

"Could you let Claire make things with the hammer and saw?"

Now he seemed confused. "Is this for a girl to do?"

"Very much so. It will help her coordination and her confidence. It should also loosen her up a bit."

"Then I will teach her." He flashed his big smile, we shook hands, and he hurried out of the room.

The next day was Wednesday and Claire brought her lunch. She talked about it all morning and kept showing me her new lunch box. She showed it to the children too. This was the first time I had seen Claire communicate an idea clearly to the others: this is my lunch box and I have been asked to stay for lunch.

There was much to find out about Claire that day. For one thing, she did not know the name of what was in her sandwich. It was baloney, but she had no name for it. She did not know the word in French either. She knew the names for the cookies, banana, and orange she brought, but not for raisins. There were other words she did not know. Simple words we take for granted, like "paste," "thumbtacks," and "puppet."

Claire tried out materials for the first time. When there were thirty children in the room she took no chances. With only four, though, she rushed around fingering everything. But she wanted my approval.

"Can I play with this?"

"Yes, you can paint a picture."

"Can I play with this?"

"Yes, you can play with the Leggo set."

"Can I go in there?"

"Yes, you can play in the doll corner."

"No, I can't."

"Why not, Claire?"

"That's not for me." She was not ready for make-believe.

12. THE MORNING AFTER her first "Wednesday Lunch Day," Claire painted eight pictures, all in red paint. She was trying out a single idea, putting paint on paper. When I walked by she said to me, "I'm working."

"You're not working," said Sylvia. "You're scribble-scrabbling."

Claire kept her eyes on her red picture and repeated, "I'm working."

I could trace the steps to "I'm working." Her first clear statements were calls for help. She wanted to avoid certain activities; she wanted Sylvia to stop hurting her; she wanted Ayana's knee fixed and her tears dried. She was talking to me.

But the day Claire stayed for lunch she spoke directly to the children. She saw herself as part of a special group, the group that brought lunch boxes: I have a certain status now, I am staying for lunch.

With "I'm working" a new level was reached. It said, I have found out what children do in school. I have something I can do now. I can paint as many pictures as I wish. I will decide what color to use and what form the picture will take.

For several weeks, Claire spent most of her time painting. She used one color each day. If she began with blue, all her pictures would be blue that day. One morning she decided to use every color at once, and it ended up the color of mud. She seemed surprised that all those colors could turn into a muddy brown.

In four weeks' time she advanced from three-year-old to five-year-old with her paintbrush. I was at the table when the big leap occurred. Claire had been watching Richard, who always painted pictures of houses. Except for the time I asked everyone to do a self-portrait, he never drew anything but houses.

Claire concentrated on every stroke of his brush. "What that is?" she asked.

"It's a chimney, of course," he answered.

She copied Richard's house, using the same colors and shapes. When she was finished, she brought it to me.

"I made a house. It don't have a chimney." This was the first of many houses. Hers were never as neat as Richard's, but being less conventional they were also more interesting. They had a Chagall-like quality.

There is something about drawing a house that intrigues many children. When they find out how to make one, they generally want to keep making houses for a long while. This was what Claire did, until the Wednesday afternoon she discovered she could draw a whole person instead of her customary unattached face. She found out about bodies and

eyelashes at the same time. Joyce had stayed for
lunch too that day. She and Claire were drawing
with crayons while I mended old books. She looked
at Claire's paper and said, "Girl, how come you
never make a body? You only make the head. You
want me to show you?" Joyce was black, and she
usually called other black girls "girl."

Joyce made her drawing in a way that always
seems strange to me, though each class has a few
people who draw this way. She began with the feet
first and drew upwards. The hair came last and she
spent a lot of time on hair and eyelashes. Her pictures were quite mature, well beyond Claire's ability. Claire tried to copy Joyce, but could not even
make the feet. However, she did not become dis-
couraged, which is a valuable piece of information
to have about a child. Finally she drew one of her
big round faces and added lines for the body, arms,
and legs. This pleased her. She made another figure
just like the first. Then she drew eyelashes with
great care.

"What this is called?" she asked me.

"They're called eyelashes."

"Eyelashes, eyelashes, eyelashes." She kept repeating the word as if she had never heard one
more interesting.

This seemed to give Joyce an idea. "Hey, girl,
let's play in the doll house. I'll be the mother. You
be the baby."

Claire hesitated, but Joyce took her by the hand
and led her to the doll crib. "Lie down, baby. Pretend you're crying because you're sick and you

don't have no daddy. I'm going to make some medicine."

Claire allowed herself to be put to bed. She didn't cry but she did put her thumb in her mouth. When Joyce brought her the medicine, Claire said with great seriousness, "I'm the baby."

The next day, Claire did not go into the doll corner. It was too crowded. Joyce did not ask her to play, probably because it was more fun to play with the others.

The art table is a good place to be if you are not ready for complicated social problems. You can first gain courage with materials you are able to control, and then transfer these feelings to the social arena.

Claire's pictures had gone into a new multimedium stage.

"Claire, I see you're making a collage," I said. She looked surprised.

"You're glueing pieces of things on your painting. We call that a collage."

"I call it a glue painting," she said.

"No," said Anna, with authority. "A glue painting is when you mix glue and paint together."

"This is a collage," said Claire, looking at me to see if she said it right.

I nodded. "But glue painting could be a good name for it too, Claire."

Anna was a stickler for propriety. "It's a collage."

"Right," said Claire, smiling widely. "Collage." She found it pleasant to agree with Anna.

Claire was taking big steps every day, but many of her reactions continued to confuse me. When I asked everyone to bring an apple to school so we could make applesauce, she did not understand what we were planning to do. This was a math activity that would turn into a cooking session. We agreed to make the applesauce on the day the thirtieth apple was brought in. Each apple received a number and was lined up in a row on top of the piano.

Claire saw and heard all of this, but asked each day if I would give her an apple.

"I can't do that, Claire. We're going to cook these. If you're able to bring one, we'll cook yours too. But even if you can't bring an apple, you'll still help us make the applesauce and eat it."

"My mama don't have an apple. You give me one?"

When we finally cooked and ate the applesauce I think she was able to piece together all the parts of the activity. But I'm not really sure.

I was determined to avoid the feeling that I must understand and judge everything Claire did. But when you lack faith in a child's ability, you show it in subtle ways. You don't introduce them to certain activities, or if you do you stop at the first sign of trouble. You avoid giving them time and attention in certain kinds of discussions. Somehow the children who excel are given practice in excelling. The children who begin slowly receive a different set of experiences. There were games I avoided with Claire. I expected failure and told myself it was best to go where success was likely.

For example, we have a game called Take-Ball.

The first week of school Anna played the game with Claire and showed her every step. Claire could not do it at all. She waited for Anna to tell her what to do every time it was her turn. Later I asked Rena to play the game with Claire and the same thing happened.

Thanksgiving was almost here and I had not returned to Take-Ball with Claire. This may seem inconsequential. I tended to exaggerate the importance of Take-Ball as a diagnostic tool, because it took more than one explanation for me to understand the game. I am not good at games. I don't concentrate on directions the first time they are given. When someone learns the game instantly, as Anna and Rena did, my mind ticks off "bright." I didn't even give Claire a second chance.

One day a visitor asked me how the Take-Ball game is played. I demonstrated it quickly. We happened to be at a table where Claire was crayoning. The visitor invited her to play. She assumed Claire knew how. I said nothing, but went to help at the workbench. I watched apprehensively from across the room.

Claire was definitely playing. The visitor gave no directions and they were each making moves at the same pace. I stayed away from the game, but when they were finished, I asked Claire if she would play with me. I felt the excitement that a researcher must experience as a crucial piece of evidence is about to be uncovered.

"Who will go first, Claire?"

"You go."

I made my move and held my breath. Claire moved quickly and correctly.

"Claire, who showed you how to play?" I couldn't accept her knowledge of the game.

"Everybody. I watch everybody play Take-Ball."

I still wasn't satisfied. Sometimes one is almost afraid to hear good news, only to be disappointed later.

"How do you know which balls you can take, Claire?"

"When the arrow points to them."

I picked Claire up and hugged her. I felt wild with happiness. "You did it, you did it!"

The visitor stared at me with amazement. But Claire burst out laughing. We both laughed until everyone around us laughed. They did not know why we were laughing, and I don't think Claire knew why I was laughing. But happiness is contagious, and soon the visitor was laughing too.

13. CLAIRE SPENT A LOT OF TIME watching the other black children. She followed the activities of two girls in particular, Sylvia and Ayana, though neither one paid much attention to her. Sylvia must have appeared much like the "bad" children her father would not allow her to play with.

Sylvia entered our class during the third week of school. Her first day was a series of explosions. Suddenly there was grabbing, crying, yelling, and demanding. Materials, attention, time, and space became items of contention wherever Sylvia went. Claire stayed very close to me during Sylvia's first week.

Each succeeding day became better because Sylvia's strengths began to show themselves, and worse because her presence in the class was disrupting everything. She was quick and smart. She got the point at once of anything going on, and saw what was coming next. In the midst of her own chaos, she would catch a phrase or a new word and want to know what it meant.

On her second day, at story time, when everyone settled down on the rug, Sylvia headed for the painting table. She began to spill paints on her hands and on the table. Trying to ignore her in the hope she would join us, I began the story. "Once upon a time there was a cruel giant." I asked what "cruel" meant. Sylvia yelled out from across the room. "It means bad, mean, wicked, and lousy." Then she washed her hands and came to hear the rest of the story.

By the second week we were watching Sylvia in the anxious way you watch a bee trapped in a room. You keep an eye on the bee no matter what else you are doing. When Sylvia entered an activity the other children looked for ways to protect themselves. She had to have everything she saw. The classic picture of the starving man in the cafeteria came to mind.

One day a group was playing quietly in the doll corner. Sylvia joined them, and a clamor began. "Take her out! She's spoiling everything!"

Ayana was painting at a nearby table. She turned

and said, "Anna, Sylvia is unhappy because everyone has dress-up things and she doesn't. Now y'all help her to put something on and tell Sylvia you like her. Sylvia, baby, now don't you fret. We're all your friends and y'all going to have just the nicest time now."

With that Ayana returned to her painting. Everyone looked at Sylvia. Then Anna gave her a wig and helped her put it on. "Here, Sylvia," said Karla, "You can be a stepsister. Put on this ballet skirt."

Sylvia rewarded the group by playing nicely for twenty minutes.

The next day Ayana was not in school. Sylvia looked all over for her.

"Where's that black girl with the brown dress?"

"You mean Ayana?"

"I mean the black girl in the brown dress with the French braids and white knee socks and the dot on her cheek."

"Oh, you must mean Ayana. She's not here today. She has a cold."

"She's my friend. She's my first friend."

Sylvia continued to have problems all year. But it is fair to say that the doll corner episode with Ayana made a profound change in her. She began to act as if this classroom might be a safe place.

There were seven black girls in the class and five of them formed a cohesive unit. You could sense their interest in each other as blacks and their pleasure at running around together. There was an acknowledgment of who was black and who was white, but white children were welcomed into any activity.

This was a new experience for me. There had never been a black clique before. Black children had moved as individuals in and out of white groups. Come to think about it, a white group was not a *white* group but merely a collection of particular children bound together in friendship. Nor was an integrated group an *integrated* group. But to me, white teacher, this was a collection of *black* children.

The group revolved around Ayana. She made the difference. She really cared about people. She ran to anyone's side who was unhappy. Quickly her arm encircled the child and she whispered softly, "Tell me what's the matter. Where does it hurt, baby?" Ayana saw herself as someone who gives comfort to others. She called children "baby" and "darlin' " and it sounded natural and warm. All the children liked Ayana's attentions, but it was the black girls who picked up her loving talk and they used it with each other constantly and with one black boy, Kenny.

Ayana, Rena, and Karla came from the same nursery school. They lived in a black neighborhood and had gone to a black school. Kenny was the only black boy who came from a black neighborhood. The girls had not known Kenny before, but they picked him out as the one boy who was part of their group. They knew that he belonged. How did they know? How do I always know which Jew in a crowd has a Jewish identity?

Ayana and Rena stayed for lunch one Wednesday. They were two girls who had developed a "we" that was a black "we." They used it as I had used a Jewish "we" at their age.

We spread out our lunches carefully on the table in the doll corner.

Ayana said, "We don't eat pig. Only white people eat pig."

"Ayana, I don't eat pig either," I said, "and I'm white."

Rena agreed with Ayana. "Black people don't eat pig. Only white people do."

"My daddy sometimes eats pig," Ayana remembered, "but never my mama."

"So sometimes black people eat pig?" I asked.

Ayana thought for a moment. "White people eat pig. Mostly."

Ayana and Rena spoke about blacks in a way that was new to me. That is, they were conscious of seeing the world through their black experience.

"Mrs. Paley, remember the girl who was in the sandbox before?" Ayana asked. "She was in my summer program."

"Which girl was that, Ayana?"

"It was the black girl with the French braids, not the white girl with the long hair."

After lunch the girls decided to prepare a puppet show. I said I would take part if they needed someone extra.

Rena shook her head. "You're very light, Mrs. Paley. This is about two black Cinderellas and everyone who comes to their birthday party is black. We're only going to use black puppets."

"Mrs. Paley could be a neighbor," Ayana said to Rena.

"All right," I said, "if Rena thinks the two black Cinderellas might have a white neighbor."

"Ok. You could be a very light neighbor." Rena had compromised and we were all pleased with the way this turned out.

Until Ayana and Rena stayed for lunch in early October, I did not feel I knew them as well as I knew the white girls. I still did not know them but I was beginning to learn. I think it is a matter of clues. With most white children the smallest clue reveals a totality of characteristics I recognize. I am not aware, for example, of all the implications of a black child's saying, "I don't eat pig. Only white people eat pig."

When Barbara, who organized "the Jewish club" two years before, said her family ate kosher food, I knew a lot about Barbara and her family. From her comments about meat and dairy dishes I received instant messages about her intelligence that a non-Jewish teacher might have missed. I think I am missing part of the picture presented by many black children by not being familiar with the context within which certain simple statements are made.

14. KENNY WALLACE, the only boy immediately accepted by the black girls, came to school on a very warm day in October wearing a jacket. After a while I asked him if he didn't feel too hot with it on.

He replied, "My babysitter gave me a shirt."

"Can I see it?"

"You might not like it."

"How do you know?"

"My grandma doesn't like it."

He removed his jacket. On his shirt was a picture of a black Superman and in large letters, "SUPER-NIGGER."

Kenny watched my face and waited.

"Do you know what it says?" I asked him. He knew. "Supernigger, guardian of the oppressed." I hadn't noticed the small letters.

"Well, Kenny, I never have liked the word 'nigger.' I guess I feel like your grandmother does. But maybe your mom and dad don't mind."

"They said I could wear the shirt."

"Then it's all right with me," I said.

But it was not. I thought it was terrible. All week I wanted to telephone the Wallaces, but I always backed down. Finally I called.

"Mrs. Wallace, this is Mrs. Paley. I'd like to talk about Kenny's shirt."

"Supernigger?"

"Yes, that one."

"Did it bother you?"

"I couldn't have been more surprised if Kenny had worn a KKK sheet."

"Look at it this way. If we make fun of 'nigger,' we take the sting out of it."

"But what if a white child reads it and calls Kenny a 'nigger?' "

She paused. "Uh, yes. This could be a sticky matter to handle at school."

"For me, very sticky."

"Ok, no more shirt."

"Thanks. I'd appreciate that."

A few days later I saw a black parent I knew in the hall. Using no names, I described the shirt.

She frowned. "I don't like it. Some of our friends are really into this 'nigger' thing too, but I don't like it."

"Do you feel as I would if I saw a child wearing 'superkike' on a shirt?" I asked.

"I guess I do," she said. "Adults can handle this kind of humor but I don't think kids can. Anyway, I wish all the insulting names would vanish. I don't even like "wop" salad in an Italian restaurant."

"How would your husband feel?"

"He won't use 'nigger' even though his conversation is full of ghetto talk."

I liked the easy way she said "ghetto talk." But what if I had said it? Would she resent it? "Nigger" is an entirely different word depending upon who uses it, a white or a black.

"Supernigger" never came up again, but the word "black" was used comfortably by black children, and to a lesser extent by white children.

One day, Karla, who was part of the black "in-group," asked me if Mr. Paley was black.

"No, Karla, he's white."

"Could you have a little girl like me?"

"Yes, if I adopted you like your mommy and daddy did."

"Could you become black if you wanted to?"

"No, honey, a white person can't become black. But I think you would like it if I did."

"Yes, I would. I wish you were black like my mommy."

I thought of Michelle Parker, who wanted to look like the blond girl in the book. Karla wanted me to be as black as her mother. Black children and their parents were talking about being black because they liked being black and liked talking about it.

I had seen myself as the catalyst for change in my classes. But it was the black children who were showing the way. They were the ones who were accepting *black* and bringing *black* into the classroom.

They were also bringing in "nigger." One day Karla summoned me to the cubby room. "Ayana said a bad word. She called Felice 'nigger'!"

Felice was Ayana's best white friend and now both girls were sitting in their cubbies crying. A clay bowl lay broken on the floor.

I looked at Ayana's and Felice's wet faces. I thought, why does Ayana use "nigger" as the expletive of last resort? I wanted to ask her what the word meant. But instead I sat down between both girls and covered their hands with mine until the tears stopped. Then I picked up the pieces of Ayana's clay bowl and we all went to the glueing table.

15. FELICE SIMPSON'S FATHER was delicately balanced on the edge of the kindergarten chair.

"I feel awkward about bringing this up," he began. "My wife and I are concerned about someone in this class. We think she is having a bad effect on Felice."

It was my turn to feel off-balance. I considered Felice a strongly independent and happy child.

"Who are you worried about, Mr. Simpson?"

"Felice is afraid of Sylvia. She talks about her constantly and even dreams about her. Nightmares, really. What's wrong with Sylvia?"

"There are always a few children, like Sylvia, who need extra time to develop controls."

"But shouldn't she be in some kind of special classroom, at another school? She certainly doesn't belong in this school!"

I was shocked. I wanted to shout: this is not your business!

"No. I'm sure this is just the right classroom for Sylvia," I replied evenly. "The more I think about it, the more I'm convinced that we are good for Sylvia and she is good for us."

"How . . . how can she be good for you? And how in the world can she be good for the children? The day I visited I saw how much of your time she takes and how she disrupts everything the kids do. Everyone is nervous with her around."

"Ok. I understand your concern. Let me try to explain." My thoughts on the matter were not developed and I didn't think what I was about to say would convince Mr. Simpson.

"Five-year-olds benefit from controlled social challenges. In a supervised environment, such as a classroom, the child who learns to overcome the obstacles presented by different kinds of children can develop in confidence and self-esteem. But besides social growth, there is intellectual stimulation too."

"How intellectual?" he demanded. "I'm sorry, but how can a child possibly learn under constant harassment by a disturbed child?"

I became angry. "Just a minute, now. Don't throw

around the word 'disturbed' so easily. And don't assume that the children react to Sylvia as you do. What I call harassment is what Sylvia is getting from you!"

We looked at each other in embarrassment.

"Mr. Simpson, the thing that really bothers me is that I think you would not be so upset if Sylvia were white."

The words came out before I could stop them. I had no right, of course, to say such a thing.

His eyes followed some crayon markings on the table. "No, not so. That is not true at all," he said softly.

"I'm sorry I said that, Mr. Simpson. Look, I guarantee you, your daughter is having a good year. What you don't see is that Felice actually seeks Sylvia out to play with. She's a little fearful at times, but she wants to become Sylvia's friend. Felice is testing herself. A lot of the children avoid Sylvia. It is Felice who insists on trying to see how far she can get with Sylvia. Frankly, I'm impressed by your daughter. She is becoming a strong person."

"How can you be so sure everything will go as you say?" he asked. "How do you know Felice will not be traumatized?"

"The reason I'm so sure Felice will have a good year is because this is a very special group of children. They are more interested and involved with each other than any class I've ever had. There is no better learning environment."

Mr. Simpson's worried look was still there. He

stood up and walked around the table as if he was trying to straighten out his legs, cramped from sitting on the little chair.

"May I offer a little advice?" I asked. "Don't let Felice traumatize *you*. A child can do that, you know. Listen to all her complaints and then tell her you know she'll be able to handle all these problems, and that she can always talk to you about them."

When he left, I began scrubbing the table. This is something that calms me down when I'm upset.

16. SYLVIA AND I had a bad day. We were continually baiting each other. Mr. Simpson's words kept repeating in my head. Yesterday I had tried to make him feel immoral, but now I too wished Sylvia were not in this class. All morning I kept bumping into her poor behavior.

Twice she hurt Felice. The second time Felice had accidentally stepped on Sylvia's long dress. Sylvia fell and bumped her head against the mirror. Her response was quick and hard, and I felt as much frightened as angry. She jumped up and slapped Felice's face, leaving a red imprint of her hand.

"Stop that, Sylvia. Don't you dare do that!" I shouted. I grabbed her arm and rushed her to a chair across the room.

"Sit there! You may not slap people. Not for any reason."

"She made me fall. I hurt my head." But I turned away. I looked toward the doll corner and saw that everyone had left.

Ayana went to Sylvia and said, "Should I tell the teacher you'll be good? Did you say to Felice, 'I'm sorry'? You wait here. I'll get Felice."

She ran over to Felice. "Sylvia has to tell you something."

"I don't want to listen," she answered.

Poor Ayana. She took on such heavy responsibilities. Now she had to worry about me.

Sylvia rocked back and forth on the chair. She looked as if she might be holding back tears. Ayana brought a chair and sat next to Sylvia, but neither one spoke.

After a few minutes, I pointed to the clock to let Sylvia know her time was up. She ran directly to me and dropped into my lap. We were both glad the punishment was over.

Was Sylvia a "disturbed" child? Certainly she caused more disturbances than others in the class. I think the question is not one of diagnosing emotional disabilities, but rather must she be isolated from ordinary children because of her problems?

The answer, for me, is to be found once again within the function of play. Given that a child is not totally withdrawn or uncontrollably violent, the play activities of a regular kindergarten group provide the best environment in which to learn about people and behavior. The five-year-old who lacks controls must be given a chance to play with children who have them.

One day Sylvia was the baby in the doll corner. She curled up in the crib and cried and kicked. Then she went to the kitchen cabinet and began pulling everything out and dumping the dishes and pots all over the doll corner floor. She was acting out the role of the bad baby. She was also going beyond that point where she could pull back on her own.

Rena was the mother. "Ok, girl. Don't mess with me. You are too bad. Out you go."

"I don't want to go out!" Sylvia screamed. Rena and Ayana held on to her hands and Ruthie said, "Pick up all the dishes, Sylvia, or you can't play with us."

Sylvia looked around her and saw the girls were serious. She screwed up her face and began hitting herself on the head softly with her fists. After a moment she stopped.

"I want to play," she said, bending down to pick up a dish. Ayana, Rena, and Ruthie helped.

"Pretend we just moved in," began Ruthie. "The moving man dropped all the boxes and now we have to put everything away on the shelf."

"Let's call the boss of the moving truck," said Sylvia, beaming, "and tell him about the bad moving man."

Rena dialed the telephone. "Mr. Moving Boss, we won't pay you because it was a bad job." Everyone was laughing as she hung up. The equilibrium was reestablished.

Sylvia's destructive behavior in the doll corner spoiled the play. The girls were not afraid of her behavior. In fact, had it not interfered with their play they might have enjoyed watching Sylvia throw things about. Instead the girls forced Sylvia to change her behavior. They offered her a continued role in the play group if she conformed, or banishment if she resisted. No teacher could make this offer. I could give her approval for positive behavior or the time-out chair for harmful behavior. However, I could not guarantee a place within the group. The prize they offered was worth the huge effort it required for Sylvia to control herself.

It was Martin Luther King's birthday. I asked the children if they could tell me something about Dr. King. Joyce said, "I think he's the man who doesn't like black people."

Sylvia whirled about. "Are you crazy, girl? He loved black people! My daddy went to his office once."

Sam looked thoughtful. "Oh, then he didn't like white people."

"No, that's wrong too." Sylvia stood up. "You kids don't know nothin' about him. He liked everyone. If you were black or white, he liked you."

Felice looked proudly at Sylvia. "Sometimes Sylvia really knows a lot about things."

"Thank you, Felice," said Sylvia shyly.

Sylvia did know a lot about things. She and Ayana both were full of information about the vagaries of married and nonmarried life, for example. The knew about boyfriends and "cool cats," "dudes" and "running around."

We went to the zoo one chilly day in early spring.

We stood shivering in front of the bear cage and watched an enormous bear mount another large bear. The male looked away indifferently and the female studied a Cracker-Jack box on the grass.

"They're fucking," said Sylvia.

"What does that mean?" asked Jonas.

"You know, making a baby. Right?" She looked at me.

"Right," I said. "I call it mating, Sylvia."

"My uncle Buddy calls it fucking. Have you heard of that?"

"Yes. I have."

17. CLAIRE WAS OUTSIDE the doll corner watching Joyce, Anna, and Ayana. Karla ran in and shouted, "I'm the sister." Claire said something quietly but no one looked at her. She played in the doll corner each day now, but seldom when these girls were present.

There was a doll corner in-group. There always is. This year, except for Anna, they were all black. Anna was the only white girl who automatically assumed a place with the black girls. Anna and Ayana shared the leadership position, but Karla, Joyce, and Rena played strong roles. Though others entered the play constantly, the texture of the drama was usually developed by the coterie of five.

Their dramatic play centered on preparing and serving meals, dressing up to go to church or to a party, and gossiping on the telephone. They took care of the baby and of a succession of sick people.

Sometimes they went to funerals; there were people who died right in the kitchen. A lot of time was spent worrying about the behavior of various members of the family. There was a never-ending acting out of the trivia of family life. This group seemed to know exactly how everything must be done.

Doll corner play reveals some of the most sophisticated fantasy play in the kindergarten. It is also a subject about which many people are misinformed; they think doll corner play is "babyish." When the players are two and three years old, the play is quite simple. The doll is the important actor. Mother, daddy, and baby act out limited roles, often independently of each other.

Among four-, five-, and six-year-olds, however, doll corner play begins to probe the personalities of the children themselves. There is character and plot development that can continue over hours and days and even weeks. Not only is the structure of the family examined, but the order of the peer group is questioned. First choice to be mother always goes to those at the top of the pecking order. Mother and baby are still important, but the play now includes dozens of roles bearing on the theme of man and woman.

Far from being babyish, doll corner play at its best contains some of the freest expressions and most thoughtful observations in the kindergarten. Granted, it is mostly female play. Many boys take a role now and then, but the girls dominate the action. Male dramatic play revolves around the block and truck area. It is noisier and more physical, but it seems to provide the same sort of training ground for social and language development as the doll corner.

Claire enjoyed playing alone in the doll corner or with children close to her own level. For these children, the activity of dressing up was still the most satisfying. The movements of the others were copied, but the rich verbal content and ideas were lacking. For every success Claire had in manipulating the materials in the classroom, there was a corresponding increase in her verbal expressiveness in the doll corner; this in turn was always followed by a new discovery or new skill somewhere else in the room.

I observed Claire as she watched the girls. After a while I whispered to her, "Do you want to play in the doll corner?"

"They don't want me. Joyce told me 'go way.' "

"Let's talk to them."

Holding Claire's hand, I said, "Girls, Claire wants to join you. Please make her feel welcome."

Joyce made a sour face. "Ok, Claire. You can be the maid."

I was annoyed. One black girl tells another black girl she can be the maid? Well, what's wrong with being the maid? Joyce doesn't have guilt feelings about the role of maid. I'm the one who doesn't want a black child to be the maid. Had it been a white child, I probably would have been amused.

Claire looked as if she might cry. "I can't be the man. I'm a girl. Why she wants me to be the man?"

"I didn't say 'man,' stupid! Don't you know nothin'? I said 'maid'! Maid. Maid." Joyce wagged her head at Claire.

"Joyce, you really sound mean," I said. "If I wanted to sound as mean as you, I'd tell you to get right out of the doll corner and go play by yourself. But I don't want to be mean, so I'll just let you explain to Claire what a maid does. Then Claire can decide what she wants to do. And we're good and tired of your mean voice, so let's hear your other voice please, Joyce."

Joyce relaxed her face muscles, took a deep breath, and said quietly, "A maid cleans the house and comes once a week on Friday."

"Ok," said Claire, brightening. "I like to clean the house. I'll get the broom."

I left the doll corner feeling dissatisfied, now thinking about Joyce. She was going through a difficult period, bossy and impatient with everyone except Anna. She copied everything Anna did, and it was becoming clear that Joyce was unhappy because she was not white Anna.

Joyce was the most mature of the black girls. She was constantly busy making things. She created stories and puppet shows with the same inventive spirit she used to make her huge ornate art constructions. She was a manipulator. The world, people and things, was here for her to rearrange.

In early December, during Chanukah, I overheard Joyce asking some of the children if they were Jewish. She asked me and when I told her I was she said, "I'm Jewish too. Anna and I are both Jewish.

I'm really white too. Only my family is black. Me and my sister is white."

I was disappointed. It was as if I wanted Joyce to be my example of the self-assured black child who exists happily in both worlds, white and black. And now Joyce was reacting according to her needs, not mine.

"Joyce," I said, "I think you like Anna so much you want to pretend to be her twin sister."

"I'm just sunburned," she replied.

"Pretending is all right. Really it is. Like pretending to be one of the five Chinese brothers. But don't forget that Anna likes the real Joyce, who is black and not Jewish."

She did not continue to say she was white and Jewish, but there was a growing restlessness. She spent less time at the art table and more time in the doll corner, maneuvering for position. I did not become involved until Claire was the victim.

Claire was an easy mark, much easier than Sylvia who fought back swiftly and who knew more insults than anyone else. Claire would become hurt and confused. There were many things about her that could be used by someone who was in a bad mood. She was shy and awkward. She was still unfamiliar with many ordinary behaviors and responses. She made so few demands you could forget she was there.

On the other hand, many children were discovering some very nice things about Claire. She accepted people as they were. She was always gentle and did anything one asked of her, unless she misunderstood as in the "man" for "maid" incident. If you needed a partner for a game, or if you wanted somebody to color with you, or if you were simply lonely and wanted company while you looked at a book, Claire made herself immediately available when asked. And her happiness at being asked made you feel very important.

Claire's week revolved around Wednesdays. She knew she was the only one who always stayed for lunch and this made her feel confident about Wednesdays. During the week she would say, "I'll do that on Wednesday."

Claire and I were having lunch with Joyce, Kenny, Philip, and Ruthie. Claire couldn't stop talking. She was trying out conversational gambits she had been observing in others.

"Whoever has an apple in their lunch raise your hand."

"Whoever has peanut butter raise your hand."

"Whoever has a napkin raise your hand."

Each time Claire issued a command, the children responded. She was ecstatic. This was so easy. She never realized how simple it was to get children to do her bidding.

After lunch, she went directly into the doll corner. "Everyone come into the doll corner and play with me. I'm going to give you coffee with sugar."

Joyce and Ruthie were already hammering at the workbench, and Kenny and Philip had begun to construct a building. No one even turned around.

Claire put on a big hat and high-heeled shoes and set the table.

"Joyce, come and play with me. I'm the mother."

Joyce carefully measured a piece of wood and said nothing to Claire. Claire looked at me with an exasperated look. "Why they not come?"

"I don't know, Claire. Maybe they're too busy."

Claire brought a telephone over to Philip. "When I call you, Philip, come quick. You're the doctor."

Then she returned to the doll corner and dialed the other phone. "Hello, doctor. Hello, hello. Doctor, the baby is sick. Philip, you got to answer. You're the doctor. I just told you."

Philip ignored her so effectively I wanted to shout, "Answer the phone!" But I thought better of it. Let Claire see this through herself.

She dialed again. She would not give up. "Doctor, doctor, the baby is crying. She has a cold. Philip, pick up the telephone. It's ringing."

Joyce ran into the block corner. "Philip, will you pick up the phone? Are you deaf?"

Philip turned around very deliberately and lifted the receiver. "Stop bothering me, Claire. I don't want to play with you. Leave me alone. I never want to play with you!" He said this in such a loud, angry voice, we all stopped our activities and looked at him. Claire turned to me and said, "But I told him. I told everybody. I'm the mother. I said to come have coffee. And the baby is sick, too." She stood in the middle of the doll house, bewildered.

All of a sudden, we heard "ring . . . ring . . . ring." It was Joyce dialing the phone. Claire looked at Joyce not knowing what she should do.

"Answer it," Joyce whispered.

"Hello," said Claire tentatively without picking up the receiver.

"Hello, this is Dr. Brown. I heard your baby is sick. Do you want a lady doctor?"

Claire burst into smiles. She reached for the phone so fast, she knocked it over. "Hello, Dr. Brown. Come quick. Bring medicine."

Joyce sat down next to the doll and examined it with the stethoscope. "Give her eight vitamins daily."

"Ok, Dr. Brown. Joyce, are you my friend now?"

Joyce was at the little sink filling a cup with water. She did not answer.

"Now you are my friend, Joyce?"

"Ok, ok. I'm your friend."

18. SYLVIA WAS COVERING a large box with orange paint. "I'm going to make me a doll house with purple curtains." She had a piece of purple felt from our collage box. "Ayana, you can play with this when I'm finished."

Sylvia spent almost half of every morning with art materials. She still did a lot of pouring and mixing of gooey concoctions, but once a day she emerged with a "finished" product that gave her much pleasure. She was teaching herself to concentrate by working at the art table. Her attention span for stories and dramatics had lengthened too, but the change began to take place as she learned to play with materials on her own. This could be said of most of the children in the class, but with Sylvia the contrast was quite dramatic.

One day Sylvia was absent. Midway through the morning Joyce said, "Hey, where's Sylvia?"

"She's sick," I told her. "Her mother thinks she has the flu."

"Good," said Joyce. "I hope she never comes back."

"Hold on, Joyce." I felt that old annoyance with Joyce that came upon me whenever she expressed her feelings too honestly. "Look, I know Sylvia used to spoil some of your activities when she first came, but she's been doing fine lately."

"Mrs. Paley, I'm not saying you're wrong," Joyce said, measuring her words carefully. "I'm just saying I does not agree with you. No, not at all and no way!"

"I agree with Joyce," came an uncertain voice from the doll corner. It was Ayana.

"Do you feel that way too, Ayana?" I asked.

Ayana was not used to expressing negative opinions to adults. But Joyce had been setting a good example of independent thinking.

"Sylvia does spoil lots of things," Ayana said.

"I think so too," Philip came over with a half-made Superman costume. "I hope she stays away until the summer."

"Now wait a minute, everyone," I said. "I agree we've all been bothered by Sylvia sometimes."

"Not sometimes," shouted Joyce. "All the time!"

There was nothing unusual about this conversation. The black girls often discussed Sylvia. They enjoyed her uninhibited vitality but they worried about identifying too closely with her. She acted out a lot of infantile behavior that alternately fascinated and inhibited them. She demanded that they all be "stepsisters," and she played out her roles in the doll corner with fierce attention to the sounds of the ghetto. Sylvia, more than anyone, knew those sounds, for she had been a foster child in three different ghetto homes.

The girls were reflecting more than their concern about Sylvia. There were changes taking place in the doll corner and nobody was entirely satisfied. The black in-group now seemed to have exclusive rights there. When they occupied the space most white girls stayed out. Anna remained an exception, but even she was playing there less often.

One morning, a group lead by Anna and, except for Joyce, composed of white girls, brought pillows and blankets, dishes and pots, over to the block area and set up housekeeping. The big blocks, normally used for the Sears Tower or for Bat caves and Superman hideouts, became the rooms of a house. No one seemed to have planned the move. It just happened, and the next day it happened again. We had Jim Crow doll corners.

I felt certain that the black girls had not pushed the white girls out. They left because they were uncomfortable. They did not have that sense of belonging that is essential in a good play situation.

There were several possible explanations. More and more the black girls were acting out a particularly black-oriented drama. The dialect was fast-paced and exaggerated. The mother was nearly always black. In addition, Sylvia had been spending more time in the doll corner, and there were changes in the tone of the groups. There was more arguing, which was in part a mimicking of the sounds of adults arguing. But there was also more real dissension over how the play should go and who should act certain roles. A "baby" was always crying; "mama" was forever shouting. Someone always needed consolation. There was more strained laughter of the kind that becomes louder and louder until there is no humor left but only shouting. And there was an increase in water spilling and a state of messiness that often leads to a lower, more infantile level of social interaction.

It was easy to blame Sylvia. Her sharp-angled movements and defensive verbal reactions brought her instant attention. But it was Joyce who provoked her. She did not like Sylvia and challenged her constantly. When Joyce moved out of the doll corner and into the block area, both groups became more peaceful. The fact was that Joyce played more like Anna, which is to say more constructively, when the group was white, and more like Sylvia, defensively, when the group was black.

It occurred to me that the boys were having no such problems. Quite the contrary. This group of boys played together on a higher level than is usually the case in kindergarten, and there was certainly no racial separation. Most of the boys, black and white, shared an interest in the superheroes of the television world. They made costumes together and fought criminals together. They found ways to compromise when one group wanted Spiderman to be the "boss" and another preferred Batman. Despite the greater degree of aggressiveness built in to this sort of dramatic play, the atmosphere was seldom combative.

There were two major differences that I could see between the boys' and girls' play. The boys were more physically active and they also spent more time making the costumes required for the action. The construction of costumes, in fact, was taking up more time than the dramatic play. There were capes, masks, swords, belts, badges, and intercom systems to be made each day, since nothing ever lasted more than a single day. Costume design had become a big new enterprise. There seemed to be a correlation between costume making and social behavior. Superman play in the kindergarten is as old as television, but this was the first group I had seen to put so much time into costume production. It was also the group of boys with the highest level of social interaction.

The girls were less physically active and spent relatively little time making costumes for role playing. They became quite involved at the art tables, but their projects were usually not related to doll corner dramatic play. The doll corner was full of old dress-up clothes for girls, and the need to make costumes was not very strong. I imagine that if the room contained a number of store-bought Superman costumes the experience of the boys might be quite different. They might even spend a lot of time fighting over possession of the costumes.

It would be easy to increase the physical activity level in the classroom. There was an empty room on the second floor which we sometimes used for tumbling and gymnastics. We could take an exercise break everyday. Often the girls objected to going, insisting that they were doing something that could not be interrupted. Nonetheless, if the girls needed more running and jumping as an outlet for social and physical tensions, the change would be a good thing.

As for costume making, I sat down one day to make a crown of flowers. Rena was the first to notice. I was measuring the crown to fit my head.

"Why are you making that, Mrs. Paley?"

"Oh, I'm just in the mood to make myself a pretty flower hat," I answered. "When I finish this, I might make a belt."

"How about a silver belt?" Karla suggested. "I'll go see if there's any silver foil left. Hey, I'm going to make *me* a silver belt."

I made no suggestions to anyone to join me, but kept adding bits and pieces to my hat. By the time I put it on, the work area was full of girls and boys, all busy making things to wear. As in the case of the Superman costumes, the act of construction became more important than the social-dramatic play that followed.

I could see that the operation involved in creating the materials for play often led to more mature social behavior. It is as if the establishment of self-identity that accompanies the role of craftsman makes it less necessary to use the social arena for combat.

The "exercise break," as we began to call it, became part of our routine. Besides the obvious fact that physical exercise is to be encouraged for its own sake, the interval served to redistribute social groupings during the second half of the morning.

However, the doll corner remained the center of black female activity. The white girls often found themselves observers of fantasies much like their own, but acted out in a dialect and style that seemed very private.

Now the question is, what is the question? Is the problem that a group of white girls suddenly feels like a minority in a certain activity? Am I concerned because there is one nonintegrated area in the room?

Segregated activity was not a new phenomenon. There was a group of white girls, several years before, who dominated the doll corner. These girls came from academic families and were bright and verbal. They monopolized every activity they entered. In fact, they wouldn't become involved unless they could be the governing body. I never identified them as a "white" group; I didn't think of the problem in terms of racial integration. But these girls had been together in nursery school for two years and they were in-bred. They were not willing to take chances with other children, white or black. There was too much emphasis on being right and too much anxiety in being judged wrong. Perhaps it was this anxiety which made these girls cling to each other all year. Or maybe they were just used to each other and could finish each other's sentences.

Another group that monopolized a large area was one of restless and aggressive boys. I kept moving the block area that year in hope of finding the best way to contain the noise. The boys were both white and black and had in common a pronounced social immaturity. They could never agree on anything, except that they wanted to play with blocks all day. Other children stayed out of the block area because of the erratic nature of the play.

Does the majority role of black children in an activity point to more serious issues than other kinds of exclusivity in young social groups? Each group seems to be seeking an identity. A special quality of the kindergarten year is that children begin to awaken to the need to be part of a group.

When I was young, there was an ethnic joke in my family. It contained serious overtones. No matter what news was reported, the question asked was, "Is it good for the Jews?" I have always understood that my identity as a Jew was the most important part of my total identity.

Perhaps these black girls have heard the unspoken question, is it good for me, a black girl? By their actions they have answered: yes, it is good for me to be with other black girls right now. I feel safest with them.

19. I THOUGHT A LOT about Anna. She was the only girl in the class who played with equal confidence and pleasure in both white and black groups. What was it about Anna that made the things she did seem so interesting? She became a leader in almost every activity she joined.

Anna handled her role with ease and quiet authority, but a leader sometimes turns into a boss. Perhaps it is a signal that the leader needs to withdraw for a while. This is what Anna did. She had gone to the block area to begin a house of her own. Of course, a crowd of girls joined her. She was again the leader and had to make decisions and tell people what to do. She was becoming bossier and arguing more, two familiar reactions to excessive pressure.

Then one day she kept everyone out of her house. "I want to be alone in this house. I don't want company," Anna said.

"How about me?" asked Joyce. "Can't I come in?"

"No, I don't want company," she repeated.

The children stood around for a while and watched Anna all by herself in a house of blocks. She was busy answering the phone and writing messages. She was acting something out, but nobody knew what it was.

With most of the girls in the block area, the boys took their superhero play into the doll corner. Sylvia and Claire were in the doll corner and they were happy to welcome the boys. The newcomers brought with them a sturdy plot, to which the two girls added the roles of mother, daddy, and baby.

"Honey," asked Sylvia, "are you Clark Kent now or Superman?"

"I'm Clark Kent," Philip said.

"Can Clark Kent be a daddy?" Sylvia wanted to know.

"He *is* a daddy," Kenny said. "Jimmy Olson is his son."

"Ok, Daddy, honey. Come have your pizza. I made it just the way you like it."

"I have to eat fast. I'm waiting for Commissioner Gordon, and here he comes now!"

The boys were finishing their costumes. The "waiting for Commissioner Gordon" gambit was often used to stall the action. There was a new person among the boys and they appeared pleased. Anna had left her house in the block corner and was making a Superwoman costume on a little clothespin doll.

"Are you going to be a superhero today, Anna?" I asked.

"I'm Superwoman. I mean, I'm Wonderwoman and this doll is Superwoman. We're living in the Bat Cave."

Anna had found a way to be a follower, but it would not take her long to begin adding fresh ideas to the boys' play. She was a child who needed new experiences regularly. She instinctively recognized when an activity was growing stale. As a white girl who went to nursery school with many of the white children in the class, she sought out the black girls the first week of school. Her interest in their play and her confidence in knowing she wanted to play with them made her a leader in a short time.

Anna was an activity barometer. Her high participation signaled to others that there were interesting and innovative things going on. Her choices for new activities were not haphazard. They nearly always involved different children doing different things. She reinterpreted what she found and broadened her own and everyone else's perceptions of the activity. She saw the hidden possibilities.

Children like Anna had begun to symbolize for me the ways in which the integrated school benefits the white child. Many people see the advantages going primarily in the direction of minority groups. But had Anna been in my suburban class she would have had fewer new encounter opportunities. The differences in other children's knowledge and behavior made Anna far more observant and thoughtful. If someone had a style that interested her, she adapted to it for a while. She was equally curious about a teacher's idea that seemed to have merit. But some valuable instinct taught her that the teacher's plans were no more useful than those of her classmates.

It was no accident that Anna and Joyce became close friends. Joyce shared Anna's approach to new experiences. Had Joyce gone to the black neighborhood school near her house she would not have fulfilled her strong need to experiment with different forms and ideas, no matter how good the school was. Joyce would have been in the same position as I had been in my suburban classroom. The homogenized white school and the homogenized black school do not live up to the exciting potential of the multiracial society in which we exist.

20. FELICE SIMPSON'S MOTHER came one day to show us how to make puppets. She brought paper bags and all sorts of colored shapes and materials. Her demonstration took the form of a puppet show.

"Hey, hey, hey," began her puppet. "What's the idea? You trying to make a fool of me?"

"What's wrong?" Mrs. Simpson asked.

"You gave me only one eye, one ear, and one nose."

"Well, here's one more eye." She pasted a circle on the bag and then cut out a smaller circle that she put inside the larger one in a cross-eyed way.

"Oh, no you don't!"

"What's the matter?"

"You know. You're deliberately making me look foolish. Fix my eye, please."

"Oh yes. I see what you mean. Sorry."

"The ear," squealed the puppet.

"The ear?"

"The ear. You only gave me one."

"Sorry again. Here's another ear for you." Mrs. Simpson cut a big ear out of brown paper.

"Save that for a shoe," said the puppet. "I want a second ear that is the same shape and color as my first ear."

"Look, I'm really sorry. I'm not too good at puppetmaking, I guess."

"My nose, my nose!"

"Now wait a minute," she said. "I gave you a perfectly good nose."

"Yes, but you only gave me one."

"Well, one is all you get. I've only got one. These children only have one each."

"I don't care. I want two!"

"You can't have two. But I'll tell you what. Instead I'll make you a lovely bow tie and a fancy belt."

Everybody wanted to make a puppet. After some initial chaos, the children settled down all over the room to work. Felice took her materials over to Sylvia's table and sat next to her. I was hoping Mrs. Simpson saw this. Apparently I still felt I had to justify Sylvia's presence in the room.

Later, on the playground, Mrs. Simpson and I sat and talked. There was something on her mind and she came right to the point. "Felice is having trouble with Jenny and Karen. They are being very mean to her. Have you been aware of it?"

I thought how much easier it was for me to discuss the social problems of white girls with a white parent. When Mr. Simpson had been upset because of Sylvia's behavior, I had overreacted and underconsidered. Of course, he seemed to be suggesting that Sylvia be dropped from the school because she had problems to work out. The Simpsons would never imply that Karen and Jenny be excluded. These girls made Felice unhappy, but their right to attend the school would not be questioned.

I told Mrs. Simpson that I was aware of the situation. "Felice is not the only child they bother, but she is especially sensitive to their silliness."

"They tell her she's ugly and call her infantile names. Did she provoke them in some way?" Mrs. Simpson asked.

"Absolutely not. You daughter merely appears vulnerable to them. These two girls have been together for several years. It's not a new problem with them."

I had been worried about the seclusion of the black girls, but I was so used to white girls like Karen and Jenny I paid little attention to the problem.

"But what can be done about it?" Mrs. Simpson's present concern was quite different from the one voiced about Sylvia months earlier. That matter involved a fear of the unknown. Might a black girl who fought and used bad words be harmful to their daughter? Would Felice be denied her share of teacher attention because Sylvia's need was greater?

Now their anxiety stemmed from the known. Felice was being harassed in a more familiar way. Who could not remember childhood taunts like these? Sylvia's behavior had stemmed from her own anger and confusion. The Simpsons had not for a moment thought it reflected some inadequacy present in Felice. But Karen's and Jenny's reaction was more like a snub. Their daughter was being spurned. She was not popular with two girls who "belonged."

"I've talked to Felice about this," I said. "I told

her that I thought Karen and Jenny were rude to people because they didn't know how to keep busy doing interesting things. *She* knew how and didn't need to spend her time being rude."

"Did Felice understand you?"

"I think she understood that the girls' behavior was no fault of hers. After all, it's the truth. Felice is old enough to realize that most people act mean because *they* feel badly. We have to learn early not to internalize someone else's uncivility."

Unlike Anna, who had been their close friend in nursery school, Karen and Jenny tried to insulate themselves. Karen was one of the brightest children in the class, yet she consistently rejected new experiences. Jenny was far more accepting of people and ideas when Karen was not with her, but the two together acted on cue out of long habit. How many times had we listened to Karen saying, "We don't like that, do we?" with Jenny nodding in agreement?

Karen suffered from a "phobia" not uncommon in the children of high-achievement families. Their fear is of being judged and found wanting; they use a number of methods to avoid exposure. Behaving negatively is one way to keep people at a distance.

I had been noticing that when Karen and Jenny played with black children they were friendlier and more relaxed. There was no sarcasm, no name calling, and no silliness. Both girls watched the black girls in the doll corner; they obviously wanted to join them. I tried to manipulate situations so that

Karen and Jenny could make a natural entrance into the black group. But this approach is always detected and understood by children. They know exactly what the teacher is trying to do. It isn't that that children mind your efforts; it's just that the ploy seldom works. You cannot manufacture friendships to suit some notion you have of what a child needs.

One day Claire brought a note saying that she was invited to go home with Karen after school. I was surprised. My instinctive reaction was: why does Karen, who is so bright and articulate, invite Claire who is not bright and articulate? As always, my next reaction was: why am I so full of prejudices that I can't see beyond an IQ score and perfect grammar?

Claire and Karen played together all morning. I had never seen Karen so gentle and pleasant. They played Take-Ball and dominoes, Claire's favorite games. They held hands going out to the playground, and at the end of the morning they entered the doll corner together. No one was there, and so Karen was the mother and Claire was the sister until it was time to go home.

21. "WHITE PEOPLE TELL LIES," said Rena as we were putting away blocks.

"That's right, they do tell lies," Ayana agreed.

"Do all white people tell lies?" I asked.

Ayana read my face. "Uh . . . no. Not *all* white people." She looked guiltily at Rena.

Rena paid no attention to Ayana. Instead she smiled to herself and kept stacking up blocks.

Once Ayana had said, "There are angels in the clouds blowing the wind," and I had responded, "Do angels make the winds blow?" She did not take my question as a criticism. She described fluffy angels bellowing forth puffs of wind.

When I asked her about white people telling lies, she knew this was not a safe thing to have said. There was apparently no way I could keep a neutral look on my face.

Rena and Ayana were the girls who had told me at lunch one day that only white people ate pig. What did this mean to the children? They knew many black people ate pork, and had said as much. They also knew that everyone was capable of telling lies. They were conscious of doing so themselves when a lie served their purpose better than the truth.

Nor did these sentiments reflect their person-to-person responses in the classroom. On the contrary, they were more likely to accuse Sylvia or Joyce or each other of lying than the white children. They saw the behavior of the black children within the context of their own experience and were quick to issue a grievance.

Black children, in my presence, seldom spoke of whites as a class. But when they did, it was inevitably to point to some undesirable characteristic. Any sentence that began with "White people . . ." was followed with a negative observation.

When I was little, my grandmother contributed the same kinds of opinions to my growing store of impressions. When she began a sentence "Gentiles always . . ." I knew it would reflect bitterness and suspicion. I did not like it when she said those things. Later I understood how years of pogroms and persecution could make her feel that way.

I also knew, as Ayana was beginning to learn, that you did not say these things in front of "them." "White people eat pig . . . tell lies . . ." was no different from my grandmother's descriptions of the foolish and irrational behavior of non-Jews. I had understood that these were exaggerations. The gentiles I met seldom fitted into these categories. In fact, the scandalous deeds told in juicy detail by my family nearly always involved people we knew and expected better of because they were Jewish.

But what *did* come across to me, as I was sure it already had to these black girls, was the imperative to distrust "them." One must not be too open or too revealing with those who might yet see you as a victim.

I had been aware for some time that the white children in my class behaved better when playing with black children and that the opposite was also true. Karen and Jenny spent their annoying, mischievous acts on other white children and were quite agreeable with blacks. Sylvia was far more compatible playing with whites. I, too, was more

likely to expose personal negative feelings in a Jewish group than in a non-Jewish one.

When Ayana first entered our class, I misjudged
her compassionate behavior as being all there was
to know about her. I wanted this to be the real
Ayana because I still needed to have black children
justify themselves by behaving better than whites.
As Ayana and the black girls strengthened their
bonds, Ayana began to act in more ordinary ways. I
was disappointed. Where was my perfect child?
Where was the one I could hold up to white teachers
and parents as a paragon? She never existed. What
did exist was a nice but complicated personality
who was trying to figure out a set of behaviors that
made sense in her new world of white people.

If Joyce was the most consciously assimilated
black girl in the class, Rena was certainly the least.
She expressed few doubts.

"Black people cook the best food."

"Black people are the prettiest."

"Black churches are the most beautiful."

These were some of Rena's positive views. She also
expressed the most negative points about whites,
but always in random generalizations. She was
never unpleasant to white children, only noncom-
mittal. It was the black child who could make her
happy or sad. The white child had no such influence.

One day Rena asked me why there were so many
white children in the class. The question surprised
me and I laughed. I was immediately reminded of a

joke from my childhood: an old Jew from a tiny village in Russia visits a much larger town. Upon being told that there were five hundred Jews and fifty thousand gentiles, he asks, "So why do they need so many gentiles?"

"Why are you laughing, Mrs. Paley? Why *are* there so many white people here?" Rena asked again.

"I'm laughing because your question sounded funny to me. But if I were black I might wonder about the same thing."

"I've been wondering about it for a long time," she said. "The school I used to go to had only black people."

"Did you like that better?" I asked.

"I like this school better because no one gets spanked and we can play more. But I like black people better."

"Well, Rena," I said, taking my time. "I think there are more white people here because this school is in a neighborhood where more white people live."

She looked at me intently. I thought she might ask why more white people live here, but she didn't. I said nothing further.

Rena drew only brown-skinned people. Every character in a story appeared black to her. This was even more apparent because five-year-olds seldom draw *any* skin color. They leave the inside of the face colorless, much as they leave a huge space between the strip of blue sky at the top of a page and the strip of green grass at the bottom. When five-year-olds connect the grass and sky at the horizon, or color in skin, they have been carefully taught to do so.

Rena made Cinderella black. Snow White was black. Goldilocks was black, though with yellow hair.

"Snow White can't have brown skin," Karen said to her one day. "She's called Snow White. *White,* you see."

"She's called 'Snow White' because she always wears a white dress," Rena said with certainty.

"Oh."

When Rena put on a puppet show she limited herself to the black puppets. She saw nothing wrong with white children using white puppets. She urged them to do so. That was how she saw the world. Either black or white. But separate.

I would have liked to discuss these things with Rena's parents, but that seemed unwise. Her views must have reflected strong parental feelings. Had my gentile kindergarten teacher told my parents that she was concerned because I played only with Jewish children, they would not have understood her concern. They would have sympathized with my preference.

Why had Rena been sent to a school with a white majority, then? Perhaps her family felt she would receive a better education here. Or that it was a good thing to learn to feel comfortable with all sorts of people. That was why I was sent to a public school instead of a parochial day school.

Eric Stebb's mother came to visit one day and she

brought along Eric's new baby sister. Eric was black and had the same shade of skin as Rena. So did the baby. But Mrs. Stebb was white. Everyone knew Eric's father because he was the one who picked Eric up every day. Mr. Stebb was, of course, black.

Rena approached the visitor and stared at her.

"Are you really Eric's mother?" she asked.

"Yes, I am. What's your name?"

"Are you white?" Rena asked.

"Yes, I am. Does that surprise you?"

"White people are not supposed to marry with black people. Eric's daddy is black," Rena said.

I was playing checkers with Kenny. My back was to the conversation. Nothing could have made me turn around.

Mrs. Stebb answered quickly. "There are lots of black and white people who feel as you do. But Eric's daddy and I think that any two people can become a family if they love each other."

That seemed a fine answer to me. After a long pause, Rena said, "Can I please hold the baby?"

"Of course. You can hold Maria. Come sit here next to me."

When I turned around, the baby was on Rena's lap and Mrs. Stebb had her arm around them both.

Claire came to school the following week carrying a doll wrapped in a pink blanket. She pushed the doll into my arms.

"You can say hello to my baby, Mrs. Paley. Her name is Maria."

"Hi, Maria. You're a pretty baby."

"She cried all night. Do you think she's sick?"

"Maybe you'd better take her temperature," I suggested.

"No, I think she just wanted to come to school so she could play."

Jenny passed by and looked closely at Claire's doll.

"Claire, you should have a black doll," she said.

Claire looked surprised. "It's all right. Eric's mother is white and she has a black baby. I am a black mother with a white baby."

22. WHEN CLAIRE WALKED into the room on picture-taking day there was a gasp of pleasure from everyone. She was late and we were already sitting on the rug listening to a story. Claire stood for a moment in the doorway until she caught my eye. The children saw my surprised look and turned to look at Claire. She was a fantasy in pink taffeta. Her hair was meticulously brushed back and tied in a knot with a large pink bow. All her features seemed exaggerated. Her cheek bones looked higher and more angular, her eyes were larger and her skin blacker.

"Claire is a princess!" said Sylvia.

"You look beautiful, Claire." This was from Karen, who rarely gave compliments.

Claire had been transformed in honor of our class picture. This was the Claire her family knew, but we did not. We were used to Claire who was pudgy and clumsy; this Claire glided into the room as if she were leading a royal procession. Her father's words popped into my mind. "Claire speaks good English, pretty good French, and a little Creole." He had said this on the first day of school. He had known all along what Claire was like.

Joyce and Anna insisted that Claire sit between them while we finished the story. Immediately after the story, Ayana told Claire she could be the mother in the doll corner.

"She can be the princess," said Sylvia. "The one who falls asleep until the frog kisses her."

Ayana did not want to do a fairy tale. "No. She can be the mother getting married. We can have a wedding."

Claire had been silent during the discussion. In fact, she had not said a word since she made her entrance. She walked over to the book rack and took out "The Three Billy Goats Gruff." "I'm going to be the biggest billy goat today. I told my daddy, 'Today I will be the biggest billy goat.' "

There was no argument. Everyone knew how Claire felt about "The Three Billy Goats Gruff." She had fallen in love with the book. She often carried it around with her all morning. She would turn the pages slowly and whisper to herself. Then she might prop the book up on a chair and act out the roles silently, talking all the parts in turn. When the troll spoke, she would sit under the table, shake her fist and make an ugly face.

I too am in love with this book. If I could have written one children's classic, it would be "The Three Billy Goats Gruff." It has the perfect plot with just the right amount of suspense and conflict. We often acted out the story, but Claire would never take a part. Never, that is, until the day she walked in dressed all in pink.

Because Claire loved the story but would not act it out in front of anyone, we developed some new ways of doing the story. Claire herself gave us the first way. We performed together in mime, just the way she had been doing it under the table. We used only facial expressions and body movements while I turned the pages of the book. I had never done this before and the technique excited me. We could do this with all our simple classics.

Claire became quite animated. Her features changed between the little, middle, and big goats. Her entire body grew in size. As the troll, she gnashed her teeth and shook her fists along with everyone else.

Next we performed the story as a choral reading. We had read the book and acted it out so often that almost everyone knew it by heart. We paced ourselves so we breathed with the same rhythm and spoke with the same emphasis. " 'Trip-trap, trip-trap!' went the bridge. 'Who's that tripping over my bridge?' roared the troll."

We were touched by a sense of community. Talking with our bodies first and then with one voice made us look at each other with a new feeling of belonging. No one was more affected than Claire.

Why was it Claire who so often influenced me to look at ordinary activities in new ways? For me the answer was clear: teaching children with different cultural and language experiences kept pushing me toward the growing edge.

Claire had moved the chairs away from a nearby table. "This will be the bridge," she announced. "Who will be the troll?"

Jonas was the troll, Ayana was the littlest billy goat and Rena was the middle-sized billy goat. Claire, of course, was the great big fierce billy goat. She performed her part like someone who has lived the role for a long time. It was in just this way that Claire sat down and played Take-Ball with the visitor, as if she'd always known how to play the game but was waiting for the right occasion.

Jonas roared, "No, I'm going to gobble you up!"

Claire answered, "Well, come along. I've got two spears. I'll poke your eyelashes out at your ears." With that, Claire gingerly pushed Jonas off the table onto the rug. Then she gave a shout and a jump and ran all over the rug butting her horns.

"You're not supposed to do that," said Sylvia. "You're just supposed to go and eat the grass."

"I know that," Claire replied. "But I'm doing it my own way."

23. CLAIRE LIKED TO PLAY with Kenny Wallace. Everyone liked to play with Kenny. The block corner was his kingdom. He could play any way you wanted, gentle or rough, quiet or noisy. He could go through a whole Three Stooges routine, or he could listen attentively while someone else performed.

Kenny was sure that school was invented for the sole purpose of depriving him of play. He seldom came out of the block area. When he did, it was because Ayana and Rena persuaded him to be "father" in the doll corner. But if the teacher called for an activity that involved sitting down with a piece of paper and crayons or pencil at a table, Kenny's stricken look suggested that he was listening to the jail door clanging shut.

I first saw Kenny during the previous summer without knowing he would be in my kindergarten class. He was with four older black boys, one of whom turned out to be his brother. They were at the college athletic field near our school, tumbling on a plastic covered apparatus that resembled a huge blue mattress. They took running leaps, flipping and summersaulting like divers off a high board. In his eagerness one boy might spring into the middle of another's double flip. It did not seem to matter. Either the collisions didn't hurt or the boys were concentrating too hard to notice. Even Kenny ignored the bumps.

Four more boys came riding up on bikes. They were between seven and twelve, of all sizes and shapes, and a fair match for the original group. The boys greeted each other with waves, brotherhood hand clasps, and a few rounds of "Hey, man, what's happening?"

Then the ballet began. It was the scene from "Fancy Free" in which the three sailors try to outperform each other to gain approval from the girls. Only there were no girls here.

One after the other, each side sent one of its members to dazzle the others. They threw themselves into their tumbles and cartwheels with such exuberance that often the last of an attempted triple flip would land on the asphalt. They jumped up from any kind of spill, their honor retrieved with an extra trick or two.

The boys were graceful and skilled in using their bodies. The physical confidence displayed in this free-for-all demonstration was astonishing. One of the older boys walked to the water fountain and I followed him. He saw me approach and gestured for me to drink first.

"I just want to ask you a question," I said "You boys are so good. Do you attend a gymnastics class?"

He smiled and looked directly at me. "No, ma'am. We're just foolin' around. We bin in the habit of comin' here every day in the summer." He drank quickly and splashed his face and arms with water. Then he ran back to the group and resumed his place. The acrobatics were still going on. The boys never stopped moving. When it was not their turn, they practiced karate kicks and chops as in the manner of shadow boxing.

I had now been watching almost an hour of cooperation, concentration, and self-regulation. Not one complaint. Not a single disruption. This highly motivated group was coming together on an unsupervised field to improve their gymnastic skills.

Kenny was the youngest by several years. He had been trying the entire time to execute a double flip. The others encouraged him each time he failed.

"Stay cool man, you'll get it."

"Knees back. You're puttin' it together, man. Knees back. Hey, that's a good one!"

I did not recognize Kenny when his father

brought him on the first day of school. It was several weeks later when his brother came into the room that I suddenly realized Kenny was the remarkable little gymnast on the blue mattress.

But what had happened to his confidence? Where was his daring manner and proud masking of bumps and bruises? Kenny cried if someone pushed him. He became speechless if required to perform some small task in front of the whole class. During table activities his eyes clouded over and he whispered, "I can't do it." On that blue mattress he had looked as if he could conquer Mt. Everest. School had made Kenny a timid boy.

I began to watch him closely. His confidence grew in direct proportion to the freedom of movement he had. Outdoors, where he controlled all decisions concerning his body, he was most confident of all. In our room, Kenny's self-esteem was highest in the block area and lowest when asked to sit down at a table for a teacher-initiated project.

Superhero activity was becoming popular, but Kenny watched from the outside. He certainly knew all the characters and his friends kept inviting him to join them. He simply did not want to sit down long enough to make his costume. I was sure that was the reason he held out.

Kenny's grandmother had said to me one day, after a visit to our class, "Kenny doesn't sit still for a minute in school, does he? At home he sits in front of the TV set for hours." I suggested this might be part of the reason Kenny needed so much physical release at school.

"But what will happen to him in first grade?" she asked. "Maybe it's ok in kindergarten, but I'm worried about his behavior in first grade."

"Let's not worry about first grade. Your grandson needs a lot of play time now. Be thankful that he plays so well. Anything you do well leads into something else you can do well. It's catchy."

Finally, the day came when Kenny asked Philip to make him a Superman outfit.

"Make it yourself," Philip said indignantly.

"I don't know how. It's too hard for me."

"Well, I don't have time," said Philip.

Later Kenny approached Jonas who was busy making a "utility" belt. "Hey, make me one of those?"

"Ok," said Jonas, much to Kenny's surprise. Jonas made him the belt and helped him tape it on. Then Kenny asked him for an emblem and cape and Jonas agreed to do that too.

"You're my best friend," said Kenny.

The new best friend made Kenny another Superman costume the next day. Kenny brought him everything he needed from the art supply shelf and watched the lengthy procedure. He now considered himself a full-fledged superhero and joined the boys in their pursuit of criminals.

The cruel blow came on the third day. Jonas said, "Do it yourself. I'm tired of doing it for you."

Kenny came to me and complained.

"Jonas won't even make me a utility belt!"

"I guess you'll have to make it yourself," I said.

"I can't. I don't know how."

"Well, you could try to learn how, Kenny. Or you could forget about superheroes and do something else."

He went over to the table where Philip, Jonas, and Cliffy were making masks and emblems. Kenny watched for five or ten minutes and then got scissors, crayons, and paper. He began to copy what he saw the others doing. Each time he cut the pattern he had drawn he would cut right through it. Angrily, he'd tear up the paper and throw it away. The scissors were his enemy. The paper was there to make him look foolish. Until now he had avoided these activities because he was poor at them.

Back in the block area he took out his frustrations on the blocks. He built a tower and kicked it down. He clumsily rammed his firetruck into Marcia's car. She looked at him with surprise and then, assuming it was an accident, turned away.

There was no way anyone could help Kenny. He was faced with a problem whose solution required breaking down a barrier of long standing. He could resist or refuse, as he had done in the past. Before it was the teacher's activity, but now he would be the loser.

Kenny began to sweat out the task of making costumes. Huge drops of perspiration rolled down his face as he bent in solitary concentration over his drawing, cutting, and taping. He did not aim for perfection, but he knew what something ought to look like. When a part of his costume was fairly accurate he would throw back his head and grin widely. "Right!" he'd say. Or, "Hey, man, that's pretty good."

After a while, Kenny began to invent new heroes. "Supertruckman" was his first.

"He flies all over the world saving trucks from crashing into each other."

Then he created "Superskyscraperman," who saved skyscrapers from being hit by airplanes. We all agreed that, so far, "Superatomic bomb-catcherman" was Kenny's best hero.

Kenny said, "This one saves the whole world. Even the enemies."

Kenny's discovery had gone beyond his new heroes. He learned to anticipate pleasure as a result of sitting down to make something. He had thought one could only find this pleasure on a toy truck, bike, or tumbling mattress. He saw that it was also enjoyable and relaxing to be involved with crayons, scissors, and glue, inventing things all by himself.

Kenny revealed something one day that made me collect all my old mimeographed task sheets and throw them out. I had given him a ruler and a ditto sheet that had on it squares and rectangles to be measured. I showed him how to use the ruler to measure the shapes and even held the ruler steady for him. He could not do it. He frowned and squirmed and kept looking all around. His fingers stuck together and he squinted as though in pain. I told him, never mind, go back and play.

Later in the morning I saw Kenny at the workbench. He was making a garage for one of his tiny cars. He took a piece of wood and he measured it with a piece of string. Then he cut the string to match the width of the wood. He used the string to find two more pieces of wood that almost fit the size of the first piece. They were both too long so he made a line where the string ended and sawed off the extra wood.

I said to Kenny, "You measured and cut the wood so all the sides are the same."

"Oh sure. I know how to do that. I bin knowin' that."

24. THERE WERE EVENTS occurring in the lives of the children which would bring the outside world into sudden focus in the classroom.

We had two divorces and a remarriage. Three babies were born and two grandfathers died. Two fathers lost their jobs, several parents went back to school, and three mothers began to work for the first time in their children's lives. One mother became ill and was hospitalized.

Events such as these are confusing and threatening for a while. The child worries: shall I tell them at school? Five-year-olds do not know how others might react to such news. There may be an atmosphere of anxiety at home that makes the world seem unsafe. One comes to school feeling very different and lonely.

Karla Powers was trying to tell us something. She

had been tearful and irritable for several weeks. She complained bitterly about small things. Each morning began with a statement explaining why she was angry: a boy on the bus teased her or Philip knocked her coat off the hook or someone pushed her. If paint got on her shirt she would scream in dismay. A period of crying would be followed by a period of comforting before she was ready to become involved in an activity.

The play in the doll corner suited Karla's moods. The black girls acted out noisy family scenes and set up situations in which almost everyone needed consolation. I had been watching Sylvia and Joyce because they seemed to be most often in conflict. But Karla usually received the most attention from the other black girls. Ayana and Karla would go off to the cubby room, huddle together and whisper while Karla cried a little. After a while they would come out and paint pictures or play lotto games.

I asked Karla if something was bothering her. Did anything happen at home that made her sad? She would grab for an explanation: her mother yelled at her or she had a stomachache. Stomachaches and headaches were becoming a frequent complaint.

Finally I called Karla's mother but we couldn't talk because Karla was in the room. We agreed to meet at school the following week, but before Mrs. Powers came Karla herself revealed the source of her anxiety.

Ayana, Ruthie, Karla, and I were playing dominoes on the rug when Karla said, "My daddy and his friends think I'm ugly."

"How can that be?" I said quickly. "You must be mistaken."

Karla nodded emphatically. "I went to my daddy's new place and they didn't like my pants. My daddy said why didn't I wear a dress?"

Have her parents separated? Why didn't they tell me? Shouldn't the teacher know these things?

"Karla," I said, "your daddy loves you no matter what you wear."

Karla looked all around and then sat up straight as if to make an announcement.

"My daddy don't live with us. He has a new place."

Ruthie suddenly stood up and walked over to Karla. She looked directly at Karla and said, "My father moved away too. He took all his clothes and his radio. My father is going to have a new wife."

I knew about Ruthie's father, but she had never until today talked about it. Karla thought about this news for a moment and then asked Ruthie a question that surprised me.

"Is your daddy black?"

"My daddy is white," said Ruthie.

"Is that really true? White daddies can do the same thing?" Karla asked me.

"It's true. Black and white people can do the same thing," I said. "But they keep loving their children the same too."

We said no more and continued the game. How did Karla get the idea that this terrible event in her life happened only to black people? Why did she tell us about it now? Is this what she and Ayana had been talking about?

Karla's question—"Is your daddy black?"—must have come as a surprise to Ruthie. She probably never thought about her father's color. Or her own. Now she had to visualize "white" and "black" and identify her family. She could see a piece of the world through Karla's eyes.

I thought about unasked and unanswered questions from the past. Alma Franklin, my first black student, was about the same age as Karla when her parents separated. Had she wondered, as she played with white children for the first time, whether only black fathers go away? There were several children in Alma's class whose parents were separated or divorced, but the topic was never discussed. Nor did we speak of Alma's blackness and our whiteness. I had not looked for opportunities to discuss either subject.

There had been a girl named Kim whose father came to fathers' visiting day at school. Her parents were divorced and she saw her father only on Sundays. We drew pictures to give to the fathers during their visit, and Kim's picture showed a house with each member of her family (except her father) looking out of a different window. She left one window empty. "Do you want to put your daddy in that window?" I asked. She looked at me without expression and tore up the picture.

Her father got no picture and no explanation of why she tore up her picture. I had wanted to spare his feelings. I did not talk about it with Kim later because I wished to spare *her* feelings. I didn't talk about being black with Alma for the same reason. It was obvious that I hoped to ignore feelings, not spare them. My silence communicated the impression that there might be something wrong about being black or living apart from one's father.

On the day Karla told us about her father she introduced a new theme in the doll corner. "Let's play getting divorced."

"How do you do that?" asked Joyce.

"You play with no daddy," said Karla.

"Is the daddy dead?"

"He's not dead. He's just living with someone else."

The children played "getting divorced." It looked like any other day in the doll corner because the girls usually played without a father. The boys were too busy with their superheroes. But Karla felt a difference and she smiled a great deal on that day.

After Karla told us her secret she seemed more relaxed. By the time her mother came for our conference I could give her a happier report. Mrs. Powers listened somberly as I described Karla's behavior over the past several weeks. I asked Mrs. Powers why she thought Karla believed that only black men left their families.

She laughed. "Most likely she heard my mother or aunt say 'isn't that a black man for you?' or something like that. We don't talk behind closed doors in our house. Everything is out in the open, the good and the bad. Maybe that's not good for Karla."

"I don't agree," I said. "In the long run it's probably very good for Karla. She won't bury things as I've always done. In my home nothing unpleasant or personal was ever discussed in front of us. I was always trying to guess how my parents felt."

"Well, no one has to guess with us," said Mrs. Powers. "Still and all, I don't want Karla to think that only black families have serious problems."

"She'll learn about white people's problems at this school," I assured her. "In fact, a child like Karla helps others to talk about their worries. She acts out her feelings of sadness. Other children may be covering up similar emotions and it's a great source of comfort to be able to identify with someone else's feelings."

I was sure Ruthie would not have revealed *her* secret without Karla's openness. Ruthie had talked about her father as if he still lived at home, though he'd been gone for at least five months. I should have found a way to help her bring her problem into the open before this. Ayana was better at helping children express their feelings than I was.

"How do you feel, baby? Come here, girl. Put your head down. Tell me what makes you feel so bad." Ayana's words stay with me. So does Claire's supplication to Ayana one day.

"Say it to me too, Ayana. I feel sad too."

25. THE BLACK GIRLS often called each other "stepsister." I had never heard kindergarten children refer to stepsisters except in the Cinderella story and those were not nice sisters. This was more like "soul sister" and the title conferred a responsibility. A stepsister cared and worried about other stepsisters. She was critical and loving. She shared her thoughts and encouraged her friends' emotional responses.

These girls did not believe in the platitudes with which I grew up. If you can't say something nice don't say anything. Silence is golden. Pretend you don't see it and it will go away. And, above all, mind your own business. Ayana, Rena, Karla, and Joyce considered it their business to find out everything. Sylvia was a stepsister, in fact I think she was the one who introduced the term. However, she seldom developed a good relationship that lasted from one day to the next. When a child showed preference for her, Sylvia became so demanding that the friendship quickly soured. Nonetheless, Ayana had established the "official" reaction to Sylvia. She was accepted as a stepsister but was severely censured when she behaved poorly. They were harder on her than a teacher would have been, but Sylvia knew exactly what was expected of her. She tried to conform without losing face, and when it did not work out I would help her find another activity.

Claire was not a stepsister. She was an outsider. She was more of an outsider than the white girls because they were not purposely kept out and sometimes Claire was. She asked me one day what "stepsister" meant. I said that with these girls it meant a very good friend. "I am not a good friend stepsister," she said simply.

Her words saddened me. "You *are* a good friend, Claire. You're a friend to Jonas and to Ruthie and you've been to Karen's house twice. And Anna invited you to her birthday party."

"But," said Claire, "I'm not a stepsister."

A month or two earlier Claire would not have been concerned about her position with the black girls. She was busy with new words and ideas and materials and did not think about the social structure of the class. Growth can bring with it pain. She was on the edge of the black "we," but she couldn't be a "we" by herself.

It bothered me that Sylvia and Joyce should be stepsisters and not Claire. Sylvia was unpredictable and difficult to get along with, and Joyce clearly preferred Anna above everyone else. Claire, on the other hand, was always friendly and available. She would walk up to a child and say, "I like you." She said this to Ayana many times and Ayana would smile but in a puzzled way.

What did Joyce and Sylvia have in common with the others that Claire did not? Two things, as far as I could tell. They used the familiar dialect when playing with black children, and they came from the urban American culture so that they all played in similar ways. Claire's way of playing was still rather private and unstructured and she did not use American slang. She never, for example, called the other black girls "girl," and "girl" was definitely a code word.

Color was obviously not the only factor that drew black children to each other, any more than it automatically brought white children together in friendship. But neither were speech patterns the main factor. In the past not all black children who spoke alike became close friends. I wanted explanations and labels, but the complexities of human behavior defeated my every attempt at making generalizations.

There was another black girl in this class, named Marcia. She has not appeared in this story yet, for she seldom entered into the lives of the children being written about. Marcia was not a stepsister; she may not even have been aware of this special category.

She was very young and had developed little interest in other children. She played alone or with Eddie. Marcia was a black girl and Eddie was a white boy, and they were very much alike. They played next to each other in separate fantasies which from time to time coincided and created a common theme.

They were pleasant little children, but easily overlooked by the others. When attendance was taken, they were the last ones whose absence was noticed. When the class lined up to go to the library, Marcia and Eddie would still be sitting on the far corner of the rug speaking in low voices and building their tiny structures out of the smallest blocks.

Marcia and Eddie were both early readers, a skill that seemed out of context; they were more like nursery school children. They had not got to the point where they wondered what other children thought of them or where they fit in the various social arrangements in the class. Marcia knew she was a girl and that she was black, but this information did not have social meaning for her. She saw no reason to be part of a group and there was no attempt to identify with group goals. If Eddie had not been in the class, she would have played alone. Kindergarten is, for most children, the time of awakening to the society of the peer group, but there are always children who have not yet reached this point.

Marcia's and Claire's presence in the class should have been a constant reminder to me that "the black girls" were, in fact, five separate girls who played together and copied each other a great deal. I could name five white girls who played together, but I did not call them "the white girls." I was starting to realize, with the help of a good friend, that thinking of Ayana, Rena, Karla, Joyce, and Sylvia as "the black girls" kept me from seeing them always as individuals.

My friend was Sonia, a music teacher at our school. She criticized my use of "the black girls" and would accept no rationalization or justification from me.

"You don't want to keep reinforcing stereotypes in your mind," she cautioned. "It's not fair. The next group of black children who come in will be measured against these expectations you're developing."

I argued with Sonia. "But when I'm describing a scene to you, it's just easier to say "the black girls" rather than name each one every time."

"Exactly!" said Sonia. "Easier. It's always easiest

to use a group label, especially a race label. That's why you mustn't do it."

"And another thing," she continued, "what about girls like Marcia and Claire? They're entirely outside of your 'black girls.' Marcia has far more in common with Eddie than with Ayana. And doesn't Sylvia have more in common with Jeffrey? While I'm at it, Joyce is a noisier Anna, and no one, but no one, is like Ayana. 'The black girls' is convenient for telling stories but it's not an honest way to describe these children."

"Does it sound racist to you?" I asked.

"Frankly, yes, it does. What if I always referred to 'the Jewish kids' in your class? Anna, Karen, Ruthie, and Jenny play together quite a bit and they are all Jewish. What if I consistently called them 'the Jewish girls,' which I notice you never do?"

"I would probably feel you were being condescending and bigoted," I replied quickly.

"Ok," Sonia smiled widely. 'I've finally figured out how to get to you. When in doubt always open the Jewish question."

26. SONIA WAS RIGHT. I had begun by looking at differences and slipped back into the clichés that obscure differences. "White girls" did not slip easily off my tongue as did "black girls." I saw white children as individuals. If I used the group label "white" it was to round off a generalization made about blacks.

I seldom began a descriptive sentence with "the

girls" or "the boys"; when I did I was aware of gross inaccuracies, for every group of girls and boys represented an unlimited variety of characteristics.

Sonia had been quick to point out that I never said "the Jewish children." As a Jew, I was at all times aware of the individual differences among Jews. It was unlikely that I could come up with a generalization about Jews which would be meaningful to me. When I heard non-Jews utter such indiscriminate remarks I invariably suspected them of either ignorance, indifference, or prejudice.

Yet I did not hesitate to speak of "the black girls." That this should be so affected me deeply. Knowing that other teachers also made sweeping statements about black children did not lessen my feelings of guilt.

Had I made no progress then in five years? Had I come back to the same point at which I began? Was I still so acutely aware of color that I could see children as individuals only as they came close to being my color and using my speech?

I knew I had changed, but there was a long way to go. It was time to take another deliberate step. The collective "black" should be eliminated from my vocabulary. I had never needed a collective "white" to help me identify characteristics that individual white children shared. "The black girls" was not the way I wanted to relate to Ayana, Rena, Karla, Sylvia, and Joyce.

Even now I was not being accurate. It was really Ayana, Rena, and Karla who were "the black girls." Sylvia forced me to see her as a separate person.

Was this part of the reason she misbehaved so often? Joyce too demanded a unique relationship. Her continual shifting of roles kept everyone alert. Ayana, Rena, and Karla were in the most danger of having their special qualities blurred by a white teacher. Precisely because they wished to blend into each other's black identity, it was essential to preserve their independent images at all times in my thoughts and speech.

Mrs. Hawkins, way back in my first year at the new school, had startled me when she said "My children are black. They don't look like your children. They know they're black and we want it recognized. It's a positive difference, an interesting difference, and a comfortable natural difference. At least it could be so, if you teachers learned to value differences more. What you value, you talk about." Mrs. Hawkins never intended that these differences be used to lump children together and dim the uniqueness of each child. But she knew that these differences must be treasured by the black child and the white teacher.

I had been unable then to speak of color and so I could not be a friend. Friendship and love grow out of recognizing and respecting differences. Strangers cover up. Color had been, for me, a sign of a stranger. I did not look into the eyes of strangers or dare to find out about their feelings.

I have been privileged to share a year in the lives of many black children and their families. I speak more often of my own Jewish feelings and experiences with black families than with white. It is a natural thing for me to do.

It is becoming clear why my experiences with black children have meant so much to me. I have identified with them in the role of the outsider. Those of us who have been outsiders understand the need to be seen exactly as we are and to be accepted and valued. Our safety lies in schools and societies in which faces with many shapes and colors can feel an equal sense of belonging. Our children must grow up knowing and liking those who look and speak in different ways,or they will live as strangers in a hostile land.

We have walked to Boland Pond on the last day of school. Our goldfish, Gulliver, is to be given his freedom. Anna and Claire, who are both celebrating birthdays, are the ones who will liberate Gulliver. As we walk along, Claire seems worried.

"What if Gulliver don't like such a big place to live?"

Anna says, "Oh, he'll like it. Fish like big places, with lots of other fish."

Claire is still not so sure. "But what if there are bad fish?"

"Gulliver will swim away from them. He'll only go with the good fish," Anna replies.

Claire takes Anna's hand. If Anna says Gulliver will be safe, it is so.

I watch the children as they play around the pond. They try to follow the trail Gulliver makes in the water. "I see him!" "He's over this way!" Claire and Anna have attached strings to their empty milk cartons and are floating them, like boats, in the water.

Sylvia is suddenly next to me, crying.

"Nobody likes me anymore."

"I know that's not true, Sylvia. What happened?" My arm is around her and I wipe her face with my handkerchief. I can see Ayana watching us from a distance.

"Ayana said she's playing with Anna and Claire and four is too many." The tears are beginning again. She puts her head down on my lap and sucks her thumb.

Philip sits down on the grass next to us. He takes off his glasses and peers at Sylvia through thick blond lashes.

"Why is Sylvia crying?"

"She feels sad."

Philip continues to look at Sylvia while he wipes his glasses with the special paper he always carries in his pocket.

"Hey, Sylvia, you wanna be Batgirl?"

Slowly Sylvia sits up and shakes herself awake. She smiles widely at Philip.

"Sure. I'll be Batgirl."

She jumps up and runs, and Philip follows her with his special high-pitched zooming sound that we all know is the motor of the Batmobile.

Epilogue, 1989

Ten years have passed since *White Teacher* was published. Outside the classroom adults question with renewed anxiety their ability to create a just and harmonious society. But in the classroom children continue to understand and get along with one another without much practice.

Children come together in fantasy and act out stories of friends who conquer danger and preserve dependable rituals. They examine common concerns and build worlds in which friendship and fairness are inalienable rights. Everything the children wonder about becomes "Let's pretend . . ." and there is remarkable agreement about which issues are important.

The more I study this culture the children fashion as they learn to play out the rhythms and meaning of group fantasy, the more I see that the uniqueness of every person is an accepted premise from the very beginnings of social life. The children know they are each different in style and story; they listen eagerly and identify with one another's separate visions of pleasure and pain, of strength and weakness, of love and loss. In their play, they reveal the intuitive and universal language that binds us all together.

When I began writing *White Teacher*, I thought I knew certain children best because our backgrounds were

similar, and that it was my task to open up the classroom, to explore and welcome differences. I have since
discovered that all the children have more in common
with one another than any one of them has with me.
The major source of incongruity is between their thinking and mine.

The children, in fact, already know how to open up
a classroom, for play is the original open-ended and
integrated curriculum. It is the pathway to learning in
which differences are valued and rewarded because
they enhance the creative potential of the imagination.
Children do not ask: Where do you come from? They
ask: What role will you play? The children have much
to teach us, if we but stop and listen.